Wild Spirituality

Journey to the Green Heart of Being

An Inspirational Guide

Written and Illustrated by

Poppy Palin

GREEN
MAGIC

www.greenmagicpublishing.com
info@greenmagicpublishing.com

Typeset by Green Man Books, Dorchester
www.greenmanbooks.co.uk

ISBN 978-0-9561886-0-1

GREEN MAGIC

Poppy Palin

All the author's royalties from this book will go to Animal Aid.

A not-for-profit organisation based in the UK, Animal Aid campaigns against all forms of animal abuse. It is not a registered charity, as this status would restrict its political campaigning. However, it is a highly respected, effective organisation, whose patrons include Tony Benn,
Richard Adams and Chrissie Hynde.

Thank you for helping our non-human relations by buying this book.

This book is dedicated to them, and to you.

And to my parents, Margaret and Denis, who taught me how to give.

About the Author

Poppy Palin is the author of nine other published books and a contributor to two others. These include the *Waking the Wild Spirit Tarot* (Llewellyn 2001) *Craft of the Wild Witch* (Llewellyn 2004) and *Spiritwalking* (O-Books 2006). Her first for Green Magic, *Green Spirituality*, was written as Rosa Romani. Poppy was a tattooist and a Head of Art/English teacher. She is now an artist and has illustrated two of Rae Beth's Hedge Witch series. Her website is www.poppypalin.org

About the Book

Any label sets us apart from each other and so keeps us from the truth of who we truly are. This book is about breaking free of any defining, limiting terminology. Yet because it encourages us to be our whole selves again – our untamed and eternal selves – we can say it's about wild spirituality. This wildness expresses vibrant non-conformity, not mindless rebellion. It's as invigorating as a sea breeze while remaining as uncontainable. It encourages us to manifest of our innate mysticism as nature intended, in a simple, sincere and reverential way... *for the good of the All.* To find out more go to www.poppypalin.org/wildspirituality

About the Illustrations

The images aim to be as inclusive as possible, reflecting a diversity of species with beings both seen and *unseen*, revealing humanity as part of wild life. The people depicted may challenge conventional stereotypes whilst shining with their own particular beauty. These artworks are a gentle rejection of the superficial differences we've allowed to divide us for so long. Their colour versions can be seen at www.poppypalin.org/illustrations.

*'I think of myself not as a writer so much as
someone who provides a gateway.'*

Erin Morgenstern

*'Can conformity...ever lead to truth?
Obviously not.'*

J. Krishnamurti

'All good things are wild and free.'

Henry David Thoreau

CONTENTS

'Perhaps the difference between you and me
Is that I remember there's no difference between
You and me.
Equally there's no difference between
You, me and all other beings – no exceptions!

It is not for me to tell you this but to remind you.
To inspire the remembering of your true nature

And you will recollect my friend;
Oh yes, my mysterious and beloved self.'

From Inner Guidance

INTRODUCTION
Honour Bound and Free

'Thank you…for this amazing day,
And the leaping greenly spirits of the trees, and a blue dream of a sky,
And for everything which is natural, which is yes…
Now the ears of my ears are awake; now the eyes of my eyes
are opened.'

Wally Hope

'I warmed the relic in my hand, until a living heart beat,
And the tides flowed; above, within, below.'

Katherine Raine

'You are everything. To understand is to transform What Is.'
'Zeitgeist'

It was four years since I'd been able to fully climb the great, green Tor in the heart of Glastonbury yet I had to do it immediately, regardless of any physical pain or the fact my car's temperature gauge read minus five.

As soon as I stepped out of the shelter of my vehicle the wind slapped me so hard I wanted to cry. Still I struggled on towards that dark, imposing hill, knowing it'd be even colder as I neared the summit. Impossible as the climb ahead seemed, a promise was a promise – be that to another person, another creature or indeed to this terrain... this Blake-ian green and pleasant land on which I'd been granted tenure for seven years. I'd promised to show appreciation for my term of residence and offer a parting gift so I must honour that, no matter what discomfort it caused. I needed to see it through; not because I feared some manner of cosmic retribution, but because my self-esteem would suffer if turned back now. I had only my self-regulated state of grace to see me though life and how I behaved was vital to me.

So, clutching at my gifts I began my painstaking ascent. During the years I'd lived in this area I'd shared many gifts with the land as tokens of kinship. Now that I needed to move away I wanted to show my regard for this place whilst simultaneously unravelling my energies from it. It'd be impossible for me to live somewhere without becoming enmeshed with its essence on a deep level – just as I'd meld with the energies of a human other in a meaningful relationship – and I had to act with loving care when disengaging. Like an old partner, this land would always remain with me but, like a new lover, another place was calling me with increasingly insistent tones. With all due respect, I knew our time together was over.

Ponderously I waved my walking stick before me, ensuring I'd tread on solid ground as I stepped into the shadow of the hill at the heart of the Isle of Avalon. Above me the clear sky was thick with stars, wheeling in their perfect patterns. I'd been made for this, for this particular *Now*, however long it took me to fulfil my mission…and however I hurt with the inevitable grief of parting. I was never good at goodbyes.

As I stepped with infinite care, I considered my chosen gifts. Firstly there was the offering to the *unseen* inhabitants of this special place: the native wild spirits or *genius loci*. I didn't know their names but I knew them to be as valid as my own self. I'd left them many tokens in the past – organic chocolate, sparkling cordial or local cider as their whims dictated – but today I'd brought an old thri'pence that'd been a faery gift to me, along with a silver sixpence. I'd already given the spirits of this land the sixpence, casting it into the River Brue – reputedly the last resting place of Excalibur. Now I wanted them to have its shining companion too. That felt like a completion to me, with no holding back. Those ethereal green beings had allowed me to stay in their area, providing me with safe homes, and I had to let them have a final precious thing in return.

Slowly I trudged to my first port of call – the 'egg stone', a limestone burr on the south side of the Tor. Carefully I made a small hole in the soil beneath and buried the silver coin I clutched. If another human visitor picked it up from the indentation in the ground it was fine – as always it was the *energy* of an offering that mattered, not the physical representation.

This act wasn't an appeasement, nor was it some form of superstitious magic, but rather an honouring. To me, my gesture stated:

'The land is living and you, the unseen *wild beings, are as its very breath. You experience no separation from the earth as for you there's no 'environment', only an extension of your own being. Therefore may you absorb the intention of my gifting through the land. This deed reaffirms my commitment to the interconnectedness of all life. I keep faith with you because my* knowing *goes beyond my material mind and my* seeing *beyond my body's incomplete field of vision. We're this place, we're one another and we'll always be so, even as I take my leave from you this day. Go well without me and within me, my beloved kin.'*

For an indeterminable moment all the memories of my communing with these spirits flashed through my head, filled with sunshine and dappled shade and laughter. But before I could relent I mentally reeled in the shimmering thread of my own energy, taking my leave. I bowed low, touching the spot between my eyes in a gesture so instinctive I'd no words for where it came. I waited for the acknowledgement – our mutual letting-go being affirmed – and then I moved slowly on to my next port of call. I didn't look back.

My second offering was made as the path curved round on itself before straightening, so that the old hollow tower loomed dead ahead. Again it was a reflection of a gift given previously. When I'd first sought refuge in Glastonbury I'd laid a treasured ring here as a friendship token to the Guardian of Place. Once I'd considered this presence to be Gwyn Ap Nudd, the mythical Faery King that legend intimated had dominion on the Tor. Now I knew that I approached a real energetic force – a non-human being – that I needn't ascribe a name to. I no longer wanted to reinforce a second-hand piece of intelligence that told me who the Guardian was, when they themselves had never claimed that name. True wild beings are without ego and know that all names are transitory. They don't solicit deification, nor do they mind from which tradition you draw their title…if any at all. As long as there's respect and understanding of their resonance then it doesn't matter.

That nameless Otherworldly presence had knocked loudly on the door of my life and whirled me around the summit of the Tor in my dreams, helping me to create one of my most popular books and a quantity of effective illustrations. Because we'd shared such wild collaborations it seemed only right that I should now ask for their leave as I'd once asked for sanctuary. So I battled onwards, each step a physical trial for me, until I felt I was in roughly the same place as I'd been that first spring afternoon.

There I stooped and pressed my next silver token into the earth. It was a beautiful and treasured item – the gesture wouldn't be resonant if the gift meant little to me. It was a representation of my one of my favourite mammals, the fox. My contribution was imbued with my appreciation for having witnessed three fox cubs playing in the sunlight on the slopes of another local hill – a privilege I'd never forget. And it fitted with that frisky, feral energy I'd felt in that place many times, as had countless others before me.

Again this gifting wasn't a superstitious magic, nor was it a supplication to a man-made 'god', but a simple acknowledgement of another energetic being. My only desire was to acknowledge this wonderfully wild *unseen* presence that'd granted me safe haven to express my creativity positively...*for the good of the All.* So, before I could lament the ending of our union I pressed my fox effigy into the soil at the base of the step. Then I bowed again while asking my leave, awaiting the sensation of an amicable parting.

Always wishing to consider the balance of a situation I'd already said goodbye to the female guardian of the Avalonian landscape. This *unseen* presence was previously acknowledged by me as Morgan Le Fey, whilst by others as Morgaine, Morrigan or the Lady of Avalon. Yet as with the male presence I now felt that ascribing her a mythic title – one gleaned from tradition and not first-hand experience – had become irrelevant. She just *was*, as I was. Names are temporary and unimportant but deep connection remains significant.

As I'd often worked with this female energy 'in spirit', mainly via inner journeying, I chose to engage with her in an internal dialogue as opposed to via material pilgrimage. This inner dialogue will be discussed in this book, as it has in my others, as a valuable part of interacting with the *unseen* in daily life. It's vital to engage in such inner work, especially if it isn't possible to interact physically, 'in person'. One of my own touchstones is *as within, so without* meaning I always aim for the balance of (apparent) opposites such as ethereal/corporeal or eternal/transient. All my approaches aim to mesh seamlessly as part of an overall relationship.

So, I'd now thanked the wild spirits of the land and the male/female Guardian presences. I'd also taken an offering of local cheese and ale to the elemental being which guarded the mythical

'Otherworld entrance', marked by the second limestone burr on the Tor's easterly slope. This elemental being was my first encounter of a non-physical presence in Glastonbury's landscape and although 'he' wasn't the most garrulous of my Avalonian companions our connection had been interesting. It was only fitting that I included 'him' in my goodbye giftings.

Yet there were two more things for me to do before I could be out of the biting wind, which, at five hundred feet above sea-level, was attempting to flay the skin from my face. The first was to put down some bread for the wild birds in this cruel weather, braving the cold as I took off my gloves to distribute it. My creature-kin always have to be included in what I do.

Then it was time for my final gesture. This was to be for my human-kin: the present 'Avalonians' and those yet to visit the Tor... those seekers with their spirits soaring from the inherent enchantment of the place.

I straightened up and faced the hardest part of my journey: the walk up to the tower of the ruined church of St. Michael. I moved steadily forward, the wind howling with frustration as it insinuated itself into every crack and crevice of my outdoor clothing. My ears rang with it as I fixed my gaze on the doorway of that imposing edifice, the only other sounds being my muffled footsteps and my blood pumping loudly. Amazingly, there was no physical person on the Tor that evening which, as those who know it will appreciate, was unusual enough. Again I'd been guided to the exact right time to be present here, unimpeded by the curious. Yet even though I knew I was alone there seemed to be an imposing figure in the open archway, cloaked in shadow.

I'd seen this hooded shape blocking the entrance of the tower before. As I observed its shadowy presence I thought back to my first ever visit to the Tor in the late 1980s and how I too had stood in that spot in the arched doorway, hoping to look dramatic as I surveyed the lights of the town below with my dark cloak billowing out and my unnaturally black hair whipped back. How things had changed as I now stood in my utilitarian raincoat! Perhaps the hooded presence was a cumulative imprint of all those who'd stood as I once had, filled with elemental magic as they felt their own wild self awakening. Or perhaps it was a suggestion of all those yet to come? Not all 'ghosts' were of the (perceived) past, after all...

Or maybe it was another site guardian; a being testing me to see if I'd be brave enough to follow my intention through? Whoever that presence was, it observed my laboured progress as I ascended the steep slope towards them. I sent out a mental greeting, hoping that they'd be benign when I finally reached them.

Yet as had happened before when I stepped onto the earth at the top of the pathway I could see that the doorway was empty. The image dispersed like apple-scented wood-smoke from the many local orchards, leaving me none the wiser. Now I could see straight through the tunnel-like liminal space of the tower to the other side of the Tor. It seemed as it always did to me, that both entrance and exit were in different energetic localities. Both physically and symbolically this place was a gateway, and now I was going to deliberately treat it as such.

Not wanting to hesitate I reached inside my pocket and staggered forward as the wind slapped my back in mocking encouragement. Entering the maelstrom inside I placed my offering to the respectful human visitors of Avalon on the ground and quickly stepped away. Behind me I heard the well-used (and well-loved) tarot cards that I'd carefully ordered being thrown into instant disarray, whisking up from the pile and briskly scattering. Feeling a mounting urgency to complete this circle I forced myself out of the opposite doorway on the north side and felt the immediate awareness of making a transition from one life phase to the next. I'd done it!

Yet in the apparent physical world there was no time to pause and revel in this as the icy blast that caught me made me stagger. Inching my way round the tower back to the path, I saw and felt card after card flicking past me. Up they rose and down they tumbled, dancing past my feet, flying over my head. I resisted the urge to reach out and catch one – just one – but they were no longer mine. I was releasing them for the benefit of others.

Yet as they scattered I wondered yet again if this were littering: a meaningful sort of vandalism but vandalism all the same? No, for I knew that each card of 'The Glastonbury Tarot' would be found by the right person and that it'd bring them an insight: perhaps an answer to the inevitable questions they had as they came to this special place. It'd strengthen their resolve or enhance their faith in their own intuition, as it had mine. They could carry their gift with them and if they chose to discard it...well, the card would return to the earth that'd inspired them; either being buried, made pulpy by rain or faded to nothing by sun. Perhaps one would make a shelter for a slug or beetle. Or maybe it'd just find its way into the town's recycling bins. Whatever each card's fate I felt that in the balance this act would do more good than harm. It was meaningfully open-handed, not careless.

As I crept carefully downwards I saw one card had somehow landed on the path before me. I'd not anticipated there being one for me to take but here it was; a token for my own journey. I stooped, palmed it and carried on, not looking back. Behind me I could still hear the cards fluttering and flitting over the grass. *Don't look back!* All I had to do was follow the silver path down into the next phase of my own earth-walk.

It wasn't until I reached my car, flushed with the achievement of climbing that most extraordinary of hills – and doing the right thing that I'd so longed to do – that I turned my card over. The title of the card was 'Progression' and showed a woman walking away from her past, treading a well-worn path on one of Glastonbury's slopes. The beauty and perfection of this moved me and affirmed, yet again, the rightness of my own inner guidance. I'd allowed my actions to mirror my internal *knowing* and could move on now, with the wild spirit's leave...and my own.

All was well, and I was All.

This introductory story describes the blend of intuition, altruistic intention, inspiration and interconnectedness that my own life – and the green heart of this book – are about. It shares a step on a journey of (re)discovery, accompanied by the beating pulse at the core of empathetic experience: our own wild heartbeat drum.

Here, then, is an untamed spirituality in action, shared that we may all come to our powerful senses – senses that allow us to both smell the roses and perceive what's authentic. Together let's embrace what we are beyond appearance, assumption and society's prescribed ideals.

Enjoy what's inherently yours and essentially *ours*. Yet which belongs to none.

Poppy Palin
Wiltshire, UK 2013

'The word 'kind' comes from the same root as 'kin' and it means to care for someone as much as you do for your own family.'

Vivienne Westwood

'Until we extend our circle of compassion to all living things, humanity will not find peace.'

Albert Schweitzer

'When we dream we appear to be one of many characters in our dream-drama. But actually everyone and everything is being imagined by one dreaming awareness. It's the same right now ... we are one awareness dreaming itself to be many individuals in the life-dream. All is One.'

Timothy Freke

'Oneness is the secret of everything.'

Swami Vivekananda

'You are your own higher power, whether you realise it or not.
Religion has taught us this attitude is vainglorious and blasphemous;
wild spirituality reveals that it's essential.
You are the Creator. As such you can be Self-serving.
You're the only one that can judge your actions.

This isn't to say you should be in the habit of condemning yourself.
Instead give inner praise for small things lovingly done.
For these are the firm foundations of a life well lived —
the touchstones of a greater appreciation.

We must begin with ourselves before we can see the best in others.
And we must see ourselves in all others before all may truly thrive.'

From Inner Guidance

PART ONE

Exploration

'All matter is energy condensed to a slow vibration...
We're one consciousness experiencing itself subjectively,
There's no such thing as death, life is only a dream
And we're the imagination of ourselves'.

Bill Hicks

'All that we see, or seem, is but a dream within a dream.'

Edgar Allen Poe

'Reality is an illusion, albeit a persistent one.'

Albert Einstein

'And how long...can you search for what's not lost?'

Nico

CHAPTER ONE
The Wildest Tale

'I maintain that the truth is a pathless land...
The moment you follow someone you cease to follow truth...
You have to question everything that man has accepted as valuable,
as necessary.'
J. Krishnamurti

'Ethics and spirituality lie at the very heart of what's good about being
human, but thinking on both has been shackled to the preposterous
for millennia.'
Sam Harris

'Why did man...wherever he built scientific, philosophic or religious
systems, go astray with such persistence?'

Wilhelm Reich

'The great Way is easy, yet people prefer the side paths.'

Tao Te Ching

Let's introduce ourselves; it's only polite when we're to be sharing
an important journey.

Who Do I Think We Are?

I'm somebody who's done their spiritual growing up in public, through my work.

Not to say I've reached full maturity, rather I'm still learning with the gleeful gusto of a child. Each of my books is a synopsis of my understanding at the time of writing and as such they're as valid and complete as I can make them.

But they do not – cannot – express everything.
Any more than my chosen name, job description, or any other appellation I bestow on myself can tell the whole tale of who and what I am.

Because I'm Infinite Consciousness having an experience from a particular point of perception.

My point of perception is currently – and temporarily in the greater scheme of things – called Poppy Palin. And you are? Well, you're Infinite Consciousness having an experience from a particular point of perception; only yours *isn't* labelled Poppy Palin, as that unique position is already taken. In essence we're each other – *we are Infinite Consciousness* – and it's only by taking a specific perspective that we're defined. By this we're able to witness boundless existence – All Possibility; All-That-Is – as an exclusive strand of being; a strand that's only an aspect of our true limitless and eternal nature.

Who we currently appear to be is just one expression of our Infinitely Conscious Wild Self.

It's hard to grasp the greatness of our mysterious Wild Self when we're operating in what we understand as 'ordinary reality'. We're limited by the filter of our incumbent humanity and so any attempt to clarify its mystery can't help but be clumsy. Yet I feel our Wild Self has a shared story that needs to be told.

Our liberating biography: our Creation Myth – something to remember our Self by.

The best means we have of communicating the ineffable is through soulful creative art and so this Creation Myth is *poetic*.

2

It's sweeping and symbolic; not strictly historically accurate and definitely not 'gospel'. It's a love story in the broadest sense as it embraces every being equally and wholeheartedly. It reveals us – the bigger, all-encompassing Us that is the Wild Self – as the central character...as well as being present in all the supporting characters, or selves. It explores how the One became many ones and expresses our yearning to return to Oneness. In this returning we'll find the empathy and equanimity essential to the continuation of life on this small blue-green planet.

We'll remember who we all are...for the good of the All.

We can skip this allegorical tale if we wish, and move straight onto the practical part of the book that begins in the next chapter. But without reading it we'll have less understanding of our own true nature and the impetus behind our actions will be diminished.

So, are you sitting comfortably, with a receptivity beyond the reasoning of jaded humanity? Then I'll begin.

Our Creation Myth: *The Wild Dream of Being*

Once upon a time-out-of-time there was a fathomless dark slumber: the Deep Sleep. It went on and on, for aeon after aeon of timeless time. It was unmarked and unnoticed. It'd always been and so it just was.

Until gradually, from this sweet oblivion, there dawned a realisation.

There's nothing to be aware of.

This realisation meant a Perceiver had perceived the absolute emptiness. Both must co-exist or there could be no realisation. They were equal and opposite; defining each other completely.

Being and nothingness. Is and Not-Is. Simultaneously. Interdependently. As one.

It was simple and perfect. It *was.* And with this easy acceptance the Perceiver began to feel around in the endless spaciousness, pushing its perception into its farthest reaches and luxuriating in

3

being expansive...in simply being. The further It expanded the more there was to explore until gradually, after an ageless age, the Perceiver realised It wasn't expanding *out there* but reaching deeper into its own mysterious being. Because everything existed within Its own awareness It was actually exploring boundless inner, not outer, space. It was aware It was limitless and limitless because It was aware.

In fact, it was *Infinite Consciousness*, deeply awake after the indeterminable oblivion of *unconsciousness*.

With this new wakefulness came the realisation that It could perceive anything – *be anything* – It wanted to. Its instinctive motivation was to be creative. For the first time Infinite Consciousness allowed Itself to drift in creative reverie, as a Wild Dreamer.

And the Wild Dreamer had a lucid dream: the Wild Dream of Being.

The impulse of the Wild Dream was to create definition from the internal darkness. At this realisation a glimmer began, tentatively at first but strengthening to a distinct gleam. It made this gleam flicker and flare, sparking in the blackness. How glorious; the dark and the not-dark! And with this thought, the first flame grew in intensity, becoming brilliant and bold. Filaments of radiance leapt, differentiating themselves from the non-light that defined them.

The desire to experience as many variations as possible burned as fiercely as the flames themselves.

Soon the deep dark was illuminated by countless points of bright awareness, blazing fiercely or shimmering subtly. Just to think of a twinkle or sparkle was to witness them emerging – flowering – from the fertile void. These fabulous luminosities spun and swam, insinuated softly and flew deftly. The creeping, leaping, wheeling lights brought new depth; new meaning.

'*I'm dreaming myself into different ways of being*' thought the Wild Dreamer, witnessing its own cosmic unfurling. '*I'm everything I can witness and appreciate. I embrace my Self in all my forms!*'

4

And with this exhilaration came the urge to push the boundaries of potentiality.

'*Why not?*' thought the Wild Dreamer. '*I'm possible, so everything's possible. I'm All Possibility.*'

So It began to play. By focussing Its intention, anything could be created. It was just a matter of varying the intensity of Its attention. But on what, exactly? What was the substance of awareness that it fashioned form from? Well, It was everything and everything was made of Its creative energy. All energy was one energy – indefinable and unified – until the Wild Dreamer focussed Its awareness, with intention.

Energy was the essential essence of all Creation. And It was the Creator.

It now realised that the faster this energy was vibrated – the higher its frequency – the less dense, or the lighter, the result. The slower or lower the resonance, the heavier or darker the result. By varying the speed and quality of Its attention a vast array of distinct colours, shapes, textures, movements and sizes could be wrought. In every dimension, on every level possible and *all at once,* creative energy was transformed into a countless variety of expressions.

For the sake of appreciating one aspect alongside another It made things appear separate even though they were really the same.

All It had to do was ask Itself '*what if?*' and a new variation was brought into being. Some aspects of Creation were nebulous, others ponderous. Some shifted, others remained unyielding. They could be bulbous or fibrous, jagged or flaccid, rippled or mottled...or all at once. Myriad expressions lurched and tumbled, skittered and hurtled in their own unique fashion; all fresh and utterly captivating. The Wild Dreamer witnessed them all with the approval of a proud parent. It was Conceiver and Birther both, as well as being Its own offspring.

It simply was, unfolding in the eternal moment. Everything It was – all It had created – existed concurrently in the timeless Now *of Infinite Awareness.*

Just as dark found distinction by the light it was especially satisfying to bring contrast. A clammy sponginess was made more itself when compared to a brittle, jagged extrusion. A floating filament was given new meaning next to an immense many-sided structure, so concentrated it could barely be contemplated.

And how wonderful – and how surprising – to witness the music that arose from this emergent menagerie. Each particular aspect had its own frequency, according to its energetic rate: its *resonance*. The slower, or more solid the form, the lower its voice. The quicker and less substantial it was, the higher it sounded. Some rang or chimed, others boomed. Some were shrill, others sweet. Each new aspect brought a new and unique note to bear. Yet the result wasn't a cacophony but a strange and beautiful harmony, multi-layered and rich. For every dissonance there was an ameliorating cadence that smoothed the edges and modulated the tone, making it all just right.

There was nothing that was that shouldn't be. Nothing lay outside the Wild Dream because the Dream was in the Dreamer. They existed simultaneously and co-dependently. They were One.

The Wild Dreamer enjoyed this Oneness, having acceptance and appreciation for everything that poured forth into the teeming ocean of Creation. Every aspect was as valuable and vital as any other. Anomalous conceptions with disturbing proportions, strange textures and indistinct colours were as interesting as sublimely elegant things. Everything needed its opposite and creations that were repellent made others shine the harder. The rough needed the smooth and vice versa. Censoring Creation seemed unthinkable. After all, it'd be Self Censorship.

But what would happen if the smooth became silkier and the rough more abrasive? How far could a creation be stretched? Moreover, how would it feel to *be* the roughness; to experience it intimately, from the inside out instead of being forever its loving observer?

There was always the incentive of '*what if?*' to keep driving

Creation. But '*what if?*' always asked to Itself, of Itself. For although It was everything, It only had Its own Infinite perspective.

What It needed were finite perceptions of Infinite Creation.

Yes! It needed dream partners that could have singular experiences, then reflect back from a particular point of view. It needed *comparison*, with critical evaluation and differences of opinion. It needed diversity and discernment. It needed the whole gamut of unique personal responses.

It needed other selves.

These witnesses would still be the Wild Dreamer – how could they not be? – but they'd be the Wild Dreamer pretending to be someone else.

It'd be acting a role in a new Theatre of Being.

The One could become one – or everyone – through imaginative role-play. Possibilities that'd seemed limitless now expanded even further with this fresh innovation.

Innumerable wild dreams would enhance and expand the Wild Dream. How thrilling!

And so the Wild Dreamer dreamed lucidly again. First It created the stage sets: a myriad of dramatic worlds and realms. Some were ephemeral and erratic, others immense and intense. There were lush worlds bursting with vibrant potential and barren, craggy planets where existence would be a challenge. Some worlds were permanently frozen, others stiflingly hot. Some were in flux, others serene and temperate. The Creator played with all the concepts until It'd developed an incalculable range.

Now for the best bit: the actors themselves.

The Wild Dreamer was elated at the prospect of fashioning a functioning life-form from every single facet of Its brimming Self, then matching them to an infinite variety of habitats. Being after being flowed forth; evolving across every level and emerging from every imaginable dimension. New varieties of creature occurred in every moment of focussed creative awareness. They swarmed, danced, fluttered and slithered. Some came boldly, fired by innate curiosity; others cautiously, with delicacy. They pushed up through virgin earth and arose from primal waters. Some took wing and others propelled through the air as if swimming. Some crawled into crevices and remained inert; watchful. From the stolidly functional to the frivolously garish, and from the intransigent to the insubstantial, all came into being. Then they either died back, unfit for their purpose, or thrived, duly multiplying into stranger, wilder hybrids.

The Wild Dreamer poured Its perception into these astonishing, intriguing forms. Its fingers of consciousness filled all Its created beings like a puppeteer filling lifeless puppets, even as It remained the puppeteer. It put on their physicality like a costume whilst admiring Itself in a new image. It was Creator and creation simultaneously, enjoying the sensation of being Itself but other than Itself.

It appreciated being limitless but also limited by a particular point of view.

Playing a particular role was enlightening and intoxicating. Even though It was used to being everywhere and nowhere at once, deliberately taking on so many guises concurrently was exhilarating. But It couldn't get carried away; It had to remember who It really was to get the benefit from experience and have the best of both – of all – worlds. It must hold the balance between its Greater and Lesser Selves even while knowing there was no other but Itself.

And yet these beings appeared to be separate as part of the dream. *The Life Dream; the engrossing game of 'let's pretend'.*

For a boundless epoch all created beings enjoyed a perceived life-experience whilst remembering their true Creator nature. They held the balance of self and Self without becoming fixated on either. They weren't *selfish* but *Self-Centred*. Just as all Creation comprised every being, every being held within it all of Creation. They were a fragment and the Whole, both at once. And because they knew they were all One they were able

8

to encounter beings that seemed different whilst knowing they were essentially the same.

Because of this *knowing* the original beings had tolerance and respect. They were part of a vast extended family and as with any family there was great love though not always great liking. They may not have understood every being they encountered but they valued them none-the-less; appreciating them for what they were beyond appearances. *They were all kin under the skin.* How could anyone deliberately harm a being that was them in disguise? Personal preferences were fine, not destructive prejudices.

Each being was as altruistic and accepting as the Wild Dreamer. How could they not be?

Some habitats may not have been easy to live in but they were harmonious places none-the-less. There was no hatred and mistrust because there was no fear of the unknown. For even though creatures lived and died, had accidents and sometimes suffered, there was no dread of death in any of the realms. All beings knew the Life Dream had perceived risks but also had an innate *knowing* of their eternal nature.

Death wasn't scary, only a returning to their true Self.

Nobody was ever really born. Nor did they die. It was more a matter of shifting awareness; of focussing consciousness back and forth: *now I am the Creator, now I'm in a particular creation, and now I go back again.* In and out like a breath consciously taken, expanding and contracting endlessly. Within this seamless round, death was just an illusion.

With this *knowing* to the fore, no being sought an external higher power. The search would've been absurd. Why search for your Self? All was well when this was understood and lived by.

But what if it wasn't understood?

The Wild Dreamer had to keep expanding and creating. To keep the impetus, it now needed something to work *against* in the created worlds. Not just dealing with hardships in the habitats but something more challenging. There wasn't enough dramatic

9

tension for the protagonists to resolve. There needed to be more friction for the fiction to develop.

Again the Wild Dreamer asked '*what if?*' What if the beings were made to *forget* who they were? Then the game would be for them to *remember;* to strive to become conscious within their life-dream. Their unique struggles for clarity would be more interesting than endless harmony. After all, there would never have been any Creation at all if there hadn't been opposites to spark it.

So the blissful awareness of the life-dreamers ended. They became comatose, that they may awaken again.

Plunged into *forgetfulness,* all beings became wretched, disconnected from each other and dislocated from their home lands. Like somnambulists they moved around but were completely oblivious as to why. Instead of reaching towards the light of understanding the created beings flailed and stumbled in their own worlds, lost and desolate. Their internal compass had been removed and they spun wildly, seeking meaning.

And what meaning was there but survival? Survival in environments that no longer appeared vital but rather as painted backdrops.

With only their body's instincts to guide them, the beings became motivated by their corporeal existence. They put themselves first, for what else was there but them and their body's inheritance; its lineage? To procreate and continue their family line was the only way of surviving death. Because death was surely an ending – a yawning chasm ready to swallow them at the slightest wrong move – and so they needed to fight for their stock to carry their story onwards. Their only hope was that their kin may get to ascendancy and prove that they had worth. To them that was all there was.

Possession became everything. The old shared identity was replaced by *every being for themselves. Mine* and *yours* became defined for the first time. The only responsibility was to the self and that which related to the self. The home area became territory, not a living place with its own identity. Sexual partners, children and dependent creatures were no longer autonomous equals but *belongings* which needed defending. War was waged continually because of the wrangling over what belonged to whom. What else was there now but fighting, feuding, feeding and fornicating? Finding a shelter, staking a claim, conquering and showing *them* – those others; the strangers they shared their world with – who was strongest was what mattered.

The beings may've forgotten but the Wild Dreamer could never disregard the fact that all war was suicide. It couldn't help but take every act of aggression personally against Itself. Yet It suffered in silence and continued to experience.

The beings now had a skewed perspective. Everything existed for their personal benefit or use. They shared their life with a supporting cast that had many expendable bit part players. They acted out their short-sighted, petty life-dramas in a limited stage-set world full of lifeless props....in a Theatre of Hate.

And so it went on. In all realms, and at all levels of existence: schism.

Of course, upon the body's demise, each being could *remember* their real appreciative, generous Wild Self again. Yet so powerful was the *forgetting* that they became trapped in the illusory Life Dream, returning to it continually to play out different roles in other petty life-dramas. Each time their awareness appeared back in a new guise they'd the opportunity to overcome their amnesia and *remember.* But because the illusion of life was so compelling they remained in thrall to themselves, and the painful *forgetting* persisted.

The Wild Dreamer kept witnessing this Great Separation even though It felt deep discomfiture at what It'd wrought. As Primary Caregiver It wanted to intervene and make everything well again yet, as All Possibility, It had no choice but to examine all sides. And as Creator It must create *everything*, no matter how unsettling...

There was nothing that was that shouldn't be. Every option must be explored.

To abort the bad dream of the *forgetting* would mean It'd never know the answer to this particular riddle. To stifle a line of enquiry – or an act of pure creativity – was to block the natural energetic flow and that would be more injurious that anything. So the project continued, the nightmare proceeding towards the inevitable awakening.

The movement towards the Great Reunion had begun, albeit imperceptibly.

Some did *remember* swiftly. The higher a being's vibrational rate – the less materially encumbered they were – the easier they found recollecting their true nature. The lower a being's frequency – the more corporeal they were – the greater their challenges. While the majority of physical beings struggled under the yoke of existence, the wraithlike, sylphlike ones reconnected with their wild essence quickly. Shaking off the dismal cloak of *forgetting* was effortless when you flew lightly or burned brightly. The clinging murk of slumber evaporated when penetrated by an unwavering inner light.

When reawakened, most of these insubstantial Shining Ones wanted nothing to do with the unenlightened creatures stuck in their *forgetful* mire. They avoided their clogged and fogged reality, not wanting to be sullied by the clinging miasma of amnesia. Yet some of these Shining Ones felt compassion for their struggling, suspicious other selves and dedicated themselves to awakening them. Danger and discomfort didn't matter when you realised your eternal aspect and so these bright beings went forth bravely, hovering close to the misery and mayhem. Their empathy was like a sunbeam to cut through the roiling clouds of the *forgetting*. No storm lasted forever and they knew the eternal light of their *knowing* would eventually pierce the gloom of confusion.

And so it was that ponderously, incrementally, the graceless beings moved towards the faint glow they perceived. It was a process that'd take generations, maybe aeons, but it was underway: a necessary, yet largely imperceptible, movement back to wholeness...a challenge that was as irresistible as it was arduous.

The beings felt a nameless *yearning* stir within them. They'd all had confusing, emotive dreams within their life-dream; night-time sleep fantasies in which fear, excitement or grief seemed so real they elicited a physical response. Yet this was different. There was an intensity in this intimation that felt utterly new to them, giving them vague notions of something *deeper* than mere survival. At first they interpreted it as an unfulfilled need. To rut? To hunt? No, it was more about expressing something meaningful. Yet what? Showing too much tenderness could make others dependent and defenceless. Caring for those outside the boundaries of kin would appear weak, leaving the clan vulnerable. Indulging the self seemed somehow profligate and caring for creature of a different kind would be degrading and foolish. What else was there to love besides physical beings? The manifest reality was all there was. Wasn't it?

Rather than overriding it, as they would've previously, they pondered this to the best of their ability.

And the more they pondered the more there seemed to ponder.

Seemingly from nowhere, uncomfortable questions arose within them. Besides the usual worries about food and shelter there was a wondering in the darkness of long nights...

Who are we? Why are we here? Where do we come from? What does it all mean?

There wasn't a physical way of answering these enigmatic conundrums; their current *modus operandi* didn't encompass abstract enquiry. Troubled, the tribal leaders needed to stop this distracted obsessing before it interfered with their tribe's potency, even its survival. It was time to think what'd hitherto been unthinkable and seek *outside* of their limited, lumbering selves. They needed to introduce another force: an external source of power. One that didn't threaten their own standing; one safe to admire that provided meaning.

A distraction.

And so the beings allowed themselves to be sidetracked from the tantalising flicker of their Oneness – away from the Source of their infinite wisdom and compassion.

Their search for gratifying good was presented as a God.

The tribal leaders used what was under their noses for inspiration. Their life was measured blood and bone, stone and loam, plus the wild forces of nature – wind and wave; sandstorm and blizzard; star-fire and rainbow. These were the things they respected – enigmatic, powerful things – and it was hard to conceive of what else a God might be. Or *where* they might be. The Gods of Thunder and Hail, Flood and Gale, weren't just omnipresent but localised – supernatural and natural both. Yet there appearances were unpredictable, except by the few, and so the beings felt a need to appease their new capricious Deities, petitioning them for their terrible, incredible displays of supremacy. But food, tools, strength and labour were all the beings had to offer up. Unless they counted life itself?

Yes, especially life! The sacrifice of other beings, and of each other, was the most precious thing they could pledge.

This act was so far from the *remembering* that the Wild Dreamer recoiled.

All sacrifice was suicide!

Surely now It should intervene? Yet It must continue to witness all aspects of Itself, including the pain of pointless murder. Maybe the beings would awaken when the nightmare was at its worst? And the wisest, kindest way be most clearly revealed by exposing its opposite? So the essential experiment continued.

Seeking divinity *out there* gripped nations and species. Putting faith in something *beyond* seemed preferable to considering the wild spirit within each created being. Deity was behind the sun or inside the ground; lurking in inky depths or elevated on an icy peak; just out of sight but somehow still present...yet never inside their own self. The beings wanted to have their unfathomable, unpredictable world put in order and be governed. They willingly abdicated responsibility for their spirituality and clutched at the straws they were offered. For although these Gods seemed to hold sway they were as hollow as reeds; empty vessels making the most noise.

But if these Gods didn't exist there were unscrupulous beings who'd willingly step in to animate them. Life was a drama and there were always those behind the scenes, waiting in the wings, who'd gladly take a part if one were offered.

These understudies were *unseen* beings from other non-manifest levels of existence. They'd *remembered* themselves and then had deliberately *forgotten* again; turning corrupt in the process. In their intentional facing away from truth, they went in search of low energies across the realms. If someone was prepared to call them a God and worship them – and, better still, offer the energy of fear during a sacrifice – then who were they to refuse? They'd no scruples. And didn't they keep their part of the 'deal' and provide something in return? They'd gladly produce a few cheap tricks, like making it snow or knocking down an enemy wall, if it meant they got what they wanted.

If there hadn't been any Gods before then there were now.

Generous *unseen* beings like the Shining Ones found this objectionable and stepped in to help. They tried to make themselves known, but it was like waving through thick smoke...a fug deliberately perpetuated by the troublesome imposter entities. The lost beings were kept in a foggy state and when they felt the vaguest stirring towards truth they were put back in line. Although the tribal leaders were partly to blame these 'Gods' were the real villains of the piece, keeping the masses in a disorientated, disconnected state for their own ends.

Because their power was reinforced through the control of the entities, the tribal leaders' narcissism grew. Alongside this came a desire for divine beings less like natural forces and more like themselves. They now wanted all-powerful, yet familiar, Gods.

As they only had one frame of reference they thought who was potent and did the creating in their own lives?

The leaders invoked the Big Parents.

The All-Father and Mother Goddess were given the attributes of any corporeal parent. They could be encouraging and accommodating or jealous and domineering. But as to incorporate the previous Deities they also had the majesty and might, fecundity and violence, beauty and terror of the wild world. They were nature red in tooth and claw, as well as being nurturing and inspiring. They veered towards the more brutal aspect because they mirrored their creator's own qualities and experiences back at them. They weren't fashioned from harmonious Oneness but from the aching emptiness and strife of the *forgetting*.

The glorious Whole became a God-shaped hole filled with misconceptions...as small as the mindset that created it and the beings didn't get what they needed, but what they were.

In theory the Big Parents were heroic and attractive but in practice they were despotic, arrogant, jealous and vindictive; expecting obsequience in return for patronage. Fecundity, protection and abundance were promised but at a price.

That was how the beings behaved so that's how their Deity acted, only more so.

In time the Deities became more inaccessible, and so more impressive. As the tribes were building on hilltops to show their ascendancy the same principle was applied to the Divine. An upwardly-mobile populace should look up to the heavens: out there...*above*. Gods should be *high and mighty*, apart from the hoi polloi in lofty realms above ordinary cares.

Perhaps if the Deities were better pleased they'd invite their subjects to their hallowed echelons when their physical end came? How they'd get to these heavens wasn't quite clear but it was an appealing idea; something to aspire to. Better than extinction with only an ancestral line to prove you'd ever existed. But how to please them more? Certainly through advanced battle

16

strategy, superior weaponry and increasing their dominion. But also through ceremonies that fitted their elevated status.

Permanent stages were needed; innovative and intimidating structures where the Gods could be honoured and their tribe glorified.

And so the great work commenced across the landscapes of all the worlds. Whole generations put their backs into projects – both willingly and under yoke – whilst knowing they'd never see them completed. They were triumphs of the beings' capacity to cooperate and pull together within their clans. An inventive, even intuitive, intelligence was demonstrated, with the graceful symmetry of Creation expressed even if it wasn't fully understood. But ultimately?

These enigmatic, awe-inspiring constructions were brilliant boasts, born of one-upmanship, not Oneness – distractions from a true reunion, not tools of remembering.

Because they certainly weren't inclusive. '*Stay out!*' the high-banked arenas, towering edifices, platforms and vast henges declaimed. '*The sacred isn't free; it's owned, just like anything else. We make the illusive exclusive!*'

Even though ordinary beings had built them, these were the dominions of the new elite; those that claimed the secret formula that would empower these places. Only they'd been given instructions from the Gods and so only they were qualified to hold ceremonies there. Yet instead of channelling sacred guidance these beings had just used their initiative, monitoring the subtle yet startling juxtapositions of the cosmos. The potency of their elegant monuments came from observation of both celestial and terrestrial events, and an understanding of the interplay between geological and atmospheric conditions. These places were open-air theatres, designed to give the best special effects available. They offered a bewitching yet mystifying experience, their magic captivating instead of liberating. They inspired awe, not an intimate connection.

Rather than being holy conduits the elite – the High Priests and

Priestesses – were illusionists par excellence.

The crowd had to be given the impression they were a part of the greatest tribe.

An overwhelming sensory experience was offered that 'ordinary reality' couldn't provide. There were enhanced or distorted acoustics that had one drum appear to be a multitude and one voice ululate on. Planets and suns could be made to appear and vanish at set times and places, illuminating or casting shadows. Moons could glide along a ridge or sink into a hollow. Burning herbs and flickering lights made the head spin and visions come. Raised energy brought feelings of elation. Wild creative power was experienced through these spectacular achievements but the impetus behind them wasn't pure. The grand smoke-and-mirrors performances lead the beings a merry but distracted dance around their illusion, not towards their true nature.

Because anything that kept the beings in separation wasn't a real step forward.

Dazzled by this show of brilliance the tribes wanted to express their superiority in other ways. Dwellings became ostentatious statements rather than just shelter. The acquisition of land far exceeded the ability to grow food. Fair bartering was replaced by the covetous hoarding of glinting currency. Extravagant garments seemed more important than merely keeping warm. Everything the beings did established a new barrier or stratum within their world; each step along the path of 'advancement' taking them further from unity and harmony.

Eventually from this selfish need to show off a genuine, pure creative expression arose. While some beings continued to produce things for admiration or ascendancy, others began to create simply for the thrill of the process. They composed unpretentious but moving music and fashioned powerful symbolic sculpture. They wrought elaborate metalwork and shaped elegant pottery urns. They wove intricate designs and discovered bold new pigments. They brought grace into eloquent being.

After a while it didn't matter so much why something was being made; only that it was.

They began to develop, not just cerebrally and manually but *emotionally*, as to create something splendid there must be both skill and feeling. They let their imaginations soar as they shaped form and wrought beauty. They pondered '*what if?*' just as their Wild Dreaming Self did. They had imaginative flights of fancy and brought those creative waking dreams into being.

They finally reconnected to their generous Creator aspect.

This reunion wasn't total, nor was it instantaneous. Rather than an immediate awakening it was like trying to stir through a doped slumber. There were moments of lucidity and periods of falling back into oblivion. Yet the inspiring creative connection remained and progressively burned through the dense mist of isolation and limitation. With this, the frozen streams of sensitivity began to thaw, seeking any means possible to surge into the beings' lives. A brighter, more caring age was being ushered in on a gently swelling wave, one that was still shallow but building none-the-less.

With this exploratory energy rising, more beings spontaneously *remembered* their true nature. They usually *remembered* by somehow seeing *beyond* the version of reality that bound them. This could be achieved through a creative reverie, and the most imaginative beings gained such clarity naturally. Or it could be revealed accidently, through pain or fasting or by ingesting a hallucinogen. Others discovered it deliberately, by *trancing*. Tired of waiting for the Priests to reveal anything meaningful, they made an inner journey to their own heartbeat drum. Through a meditative state they accessed the eternally unfolding Wild Dream, encountering their Self-beyond-self. They experienced themselves as Infinite Consciousness, recalling their true nature as All Possibility.

And so embracing everyone and everything else.

This realisation was so profound – so utterly at odds with the norm – that these beings felt half-terrified, half-elated. They'd looked *beyond* as far-seers but what could these visionaries do with their *seeing* and *knowing*? They certainly couldn't *un-see* or *un-remember*! They emerged from these experiences full of the liberating joy of Oneness and wanted to share it with every miserable being they encountered. What use was understanding if it was kept locked up inside? Light had to shine in the darkness and they were the lamp to bring it to bear! Like the Shining Ones they now knew this light couldn't be extinguished as there was no real death, only a shifting of awareness. They'd nothing to fear except for their own pain and suffering. And that would surely pass.

But despite the new creative impetus, society was far from ready for their truth. It considered itself more refined, measuring its success on its *civilisation*, not only its brawn. Sophistication was prized over the brutishness of the past. But it was all based on an impressive façade, not real depth of feeling or unconditional connection. The beings still loved power structures and inequality was rife. The artists may be painting marvellous scenes, the poets and singers uplifting the senses, the textile and jewellery workers working wonders and the philosophers discussing ideas, but all within a regulated framework. Culture was marvellous but restraint had to be exercised in case creative freedom ran rampant.

Who'd farm the land, clean the place and make the bread if all were wildly creating? Only certain types could indulge their passions. Beings just had to accept their place in the scheme of things.

The leaders of the new civilisations were as the heads of the old tribes. They tolerated creativity because it served them to do so, but distrusted independence and sought to repress autonomous visionaries. Their status quo couldn't be challenged with notions of equality and eternity. The concept of Oneness was dangerous and couldn't be allowed to take hold of the popular imagination. Customs, culture, combat, commerce, *control*: those were the keys to their kingdom. Unorthodoxy didn't deserve indulgence.

Let these visionaries be made an example of. Speaking of unity and parity was insurrectionist talk and as such it would cost them their lives.

Let them be denounced as insane; named a burden on the state. Let them be used as scapegoats for whatever ill that'd befallen society since they'd begun to spout their heresies. Let them be executed; sacrificed to the Gods who still held sway over hunting and combat, not ephemera like compassion and fusion.

And so the visionaries were killed. Yet they didn't go away. For generation after generation they reappeared and reawakened, waiting for a more receptive age to come into being. As it must.

As it did. Slowly. Painfully slowly.

And within these new, yet still dismayingly familiar, cultures those who *remembered* learned from the mistakes of their pioneering predecessors. They no longer rushed forward, offering themselves up for slaughter. They employed caution to affect change. Instead of being the individual fools that rushed in they allied with other awakened beings in secret. These groups then conceived of the best way to transmit their *knowing* to the masses.

The new mystics realised that re-accessing innate wisdom should be pleasurable and so disguised the Great Mystery in engaging myth. These epic tales could be ritualistically performed so that those enjoying the drama didn't realise they were absorbing knowledge or gaining insights. Whereas the High Priests had employed theatrics to impress and control the masses, now theatre was used to educate and liberate. A performance could be taken at face value or received as a revelation; it all lay with the witness. The key to awareness was simply being offered back.

Each sacred drama had a cast of symbolic characters – or *avatars* – that represented core qualities like compassion or wisdom. These avatars shared some qualities with the old Gods so as not to threaten or confuse the masses, but they weren't Deities. They made no demands, had no partiality and weren't fuelled by low entities. These were heroes to inspire the highest

21

good, contrasted with villains that revealed how not to behave.

The hero's journey was that of an ordinary being on a quest to find their true extraordinary selves. Within their story they had to overcome the challenges of physicality and rise above their *forgetting* to find the meaning of their existence. They may die in their attempts but their resurrection as an eternal being was always guaranteed. They were numinous but also commonplace and reachable, suggesting anything was possible. They were role models to emulate. Even the most sceptical, urbane being could relate to them.

At last the ethereal Shining Ones had a means to communicate directly with the *forgetful* beings. They helped bring the Mystery Plays to life with their bright energies: they *enlivened* them. Their subtle involvement gave the myths deeper resonance, poignancy and even comedy. *Because it was fine to take the Oneness seriously but not the individual self that tried to express it adequately.* There was much to laugh about when existence was exposed as a transitory fantasy.

Shared mirth was an aspect of manifest existence that'd been missing for so long. It encouraged the beings to drop their studied, imperious masks for a while and become less egotistical. To be receptive to a joyous collective experience, not lost in an individual struggle. It allowed them to 'lighten up', shifting the energies away from the dismal repressive vibration so long established. Humour brought beings together effortlessly and so nudged them towards the Great Reunion. It was the best medicine for the ills of the *forgetting*.

Encouraged by this openness, the Wild Dreamer couldn't resist quickening the *remembering*. It stoked the banked heart-fires of the wild dreamers. And then It waited for the reconciliation between Itself and Its individual selves which surely must come.

'Be patient you creatures under the yoke; you lands being polluted; you species facing decimation. For soon you'll be known as the equal of all others. Soon you will be as free as I originally intended. Soon...'

22

But the Wild Dreamer knew there was a wild card in the game of life: *free will*. All beings had the choice to deliberately go against the flow, even when the tide had turned.

And if any held the wild card it was the leaders, especially when they felt threatened.

The new lightness of spirit challenged their sense of control. Citizens wouldn't feel inclined to serve or be humble if they became fully enlightened. What individual would countenance their kin – their own selves, in effect – being abused? What fearless being that didn't cower from death could be threatened? Soon the populace wouldn't be sated by possessions or aggression, but seek freedom of expression. They'd shake off the bonds of materialism and the state's power would be lost for good.

The leaders knew that the old solutions for quashing insurrection would no longer work. Kill the benign mystics now and there'd be a rebellion with the masses crying for their martyrs and wanting justice. Cut back the first bright blossom, turn around and there'd be a dozen more wild blooms coming up in its place. No, the way to stamp out this dangerous nonsense wasn't by a show of crushing strength but with cunning.

The iron fist needed a velvet glove to gently gather the beings in before it squeezed the life out of them.

So these leaders moved stealthily and gradually changed their position, integrating into the popular culture. They began attending the Mystery Plays and were seen to enjoy them, laughing and crying along with the rest. Those who initiated the performances were given accolades that they'd never sought. Theatres were given patronage; actors high status. The more the leaders watched, the more they realised they needed to *own* this populist nonsense. There was something so powerful there – an energy that could be utilised – and the leaders wanted copyright on it. But they had to carry on furtively; not grabbing at it but stroking it into submission.

Let the masses be lulled into a false sense of security. Then they could seize control by declaring the Mysteries 'real'.

Or, at least, one favoured aspect. The leaders chose their preferred avatar to remodel to their own ends. Then they proclaimed them as an actual being that'd once lived and died and then risen again. Not just symbolically but literally, as a matter of fact.

So it was that a glorious, edifying and free-flowing concept was solidified into irrefutable truth. The allegorical hero became the chosen Saviour-Prophet.

The leaders had an immediate and incontrovertible answer for those who questioned this surprising proclamation. They each announced that they'd been blessed by a visitation. As leader they were expected to have exclusive visions, were they not? A vision in the privacy of one's own domain could hardly be disputed. The Saviour-Prophet had appeared to them and expressed that the masses had forgotten that their story was true. But that wasn't the populace's fault but rather the mystics who'd mislead them into believing their tale was fiction.

Moreover, the other Mystery stories were meant to mislead the beings even further. Their Saviour-Prophet's story was the only version that was real. The leader must remind their society of this actuality!

Of course, having learned stage-craft from the Mystery Plays, the leaders delivered their message with great panache. They milked the crowd, just as they'd seen the actors do. They expounded with such emotional conviction that only the hardest of hearts could've rejected their exultation.

'Our Saviour-Prophet – our Lord and Master – tells us that our nation is beloved amongst all nations. As leader of this proud land I am entrusted with His wisdom. I'm exalted and you, my friends are blessed. Let us prove ourselves worthy with obedience!'

With this the leaders raised their hands to heaven and then outwards as if to embrace the crowd, eyes brimming, voices cracking. They were a little vague on what this obedience entailed but no doubt it'd all become clear with another vision. It was the *fervour* of the sentiment that carried the crowd away, not the fine details. Who could argue with one so overcome with the wonder of it all, especially one in a position of power? Why would a head of state lie to their nation? It was clear that all the leaders wanted was for their citizens to share their good news.

And it was good news. Wasn't it?

Some didn't think so. The more awakened beings looked on with dismay at the false spectacle. Those hypocrites had claimed the precious, graceful Mysteries and in so doing had petrified them into tablets of stone. How cynical – and how tragic – to take a lyrical concept and turn it into a single hard pill to be swallowed by the gullible throng...*for their own good*. Beings that'd been entranced by allegory were now caught fast in the literalist doctrine, bound by its rules and regulations. It was heartbreaking! All the progress towards a genuine mass *remembering* had been lost thanks to this deliberate act of sabotage...

Of Self-sabotage.

Despite their almost-awakening, the majority didn't find it too difficult to relinquish their autonomy. The soothing balm of the collective counterfeit experience lulled them. It was always easier to acquiesce and be told how it was, after all. They'd elected leaders for a reason; *because they knew best.* Nationalistic pride was again stirred. And how could it not be when such rousing patriotic speeches were given.

'Our Saviour-Prophet suffered and died for us, then rose again to prove his ascendancy. Just as He is above us so are we above all faithless nations. If we believe in His power then we too will live after death and meet with Our Lord in Heaven. Only we the chosen have been offered the keys to His Eternal Kingdom!'

Now the prevailing notion wasn't *'how wonderful that we're all equal beings capable of great things'* but rather *'it's right that we alone have been selected. We're superior.'*

Consequently the leaders were delighted at the success of their wolf-in-sheep's-clothing takeover. But absolute control wasn't quite rested back.

Another tried and tested gambit must be added into the mix: the Big Parent. Only this time there was just *one parent* and it favoured the dominant masculine aspect.

'*Our Saviour-Prophet comes as a messenger from his Heavenly Father. For He is the One True God's beloved Son. Live virtuously, as the Son Himself lived, and we shall be blessed by God! Obey me as father of this proud land and you shall show respect for your Lord! But live wantonly outside the Father's careful jurisdiction and...*'

There was a shake of the head that was meant to be despairing, a beseeching look that was pained. The crowd sighed, wept and cried out praises, which covered up the general bemusement. It was better to conform than question, especially when the quality of their lives had already improved with their acceptance of the Saviour-Prophet. Each family who pledged allegiance to the new state religion was given better health care, an allowance of land, elevated status and special privileges. Perhaps there was something not quite right in the new religion but did it matter when life had never been so good? It may not be the creative, carefree era of the Mysteries but a time of plenty nevertheless. Three cheers for the leaders!

The leaders who'd helped usher in another Dark Age.

Of course, the mystics that hadn't retreated underground tried to rouse their fellow beings, keeping them from a sated waking slumber.

'*Remember the Mysteries! They taught us that no one story outweighs another; that all are equal and that all are All. We can't forget our Selves now, can we?*'

But there was usually no answer, for who wanted to be associated with a radical – and possibly dangerous – minority? It was probably best to report the rebel. The state always liked to make an example, especially when the example refused to recant. The worst punishments were reserved for those who challenged the religious institution; worse even than for murderers. For those who rejected God were surely evil and should suffer accordingly, should they not?

Because the leaders knew the masses still loved a good drama. What better than a torturous display to make the minions count their blessings? The state must control everything, even the entertainment.

Part of this entertainment was achieved by endless Holy Wars. When there were no insurgents left to fight within their own ranks, the leaders sent their emissaries to find others...*outsiders.* Nation met nation head on, each under the banner of the One True God.

'Convert all to Our Lord for the sake of their souls. If they won't be converted then take up your righteous sword, for the Godless must be punished for their sacrilege.'

The leaders ranted on. Yet they were becoming weary of performing to the masses. It was one thing thinking up convincing speeches but another to have to act them out for the herd. They were much more content to manage their armies. The leaders needed to delegate; to find envoys who'd give more compelling presentations. They needed intermediaries to intercede for the masses, just like the Priests of old had.

Whereas the ancient High Priests had used spectacle to dazzle, these new sanctioned Priests would utilise convoluted rhetoric to impress and ensnare. Only these unassailable figures could decree what was secular or profane. They'd legitimise their doctrine by inscribing it in Holy Books, using lofty language that the masses wouldn't understand. Only they could interpret the Holy Word for the commoners and intercede on their behalf.

The power was firmly back with the few.

These charismatic, authoritative Priests ensured the beings reverted to dependency, becoming less sophisticated and more insecure and suspicious. The divisions between the self and another had been blurring, and a realisation that *everything* was sacred had been dawning, but now the delineations became more defined than ever. Yet again beings were cut off from other beings, from themselves, and from what was considered divine.

Schism had its pernicious resurgence across the realms. Mine; yours. Right; wrong. Insider; outsider. Holy; unholy.

And just in case anyone thought they could step outside religion's parameters, there was another clause built in to the spiritual edict: *cosmic punishment.* Not just for life but *forever.*

The shrewd Priests used their innate creativity to dream up a negative force that would define their apparent righteousness. This evil Devil was then presented as the eternal adversary of the good God. One above, the other below; and both firmly externalised.

'There's a price to pay for any heresy or disobedience – your soul. Adhere to God's law or you'll suffer for all eternity. The Devil will claim you for an infinity of torment.'

It may be a step forward to acknowledge the eternal energetic spark yet, predictably, it was used as another divisive device. The Priests decreed that some beings possessed a soul, but not all. Those creatures that were deemed soulless – insensitive, inferior – were permissible to abuse with impunity. Souls implied status but were also a liability as they could be tempted, stolen or forfeit. Invisible as it was, a soul needed constant maintenance and guarding. If you didn't look after it as prescribed, then damage or loss was your fault.

Good; bad. Saved; damned.

Choose!

Not just now but forever.

Thanks to the will of the leaders, the dubious perspicacity of Priests, and the apathetic acquiescence of the beings, the literalist religions held sway down the generations and across the realms. The authorised Holy Stories – so stark after the original inspiring myths – were handed down as facts, just as colours or shapes were facts. They may've been austere but they were persuasive, with their defined punishment and reward systems and endorsed *rightness.* They became so entrenched as an actuality that any memory they'd once been fiction was all but erased.

The Great Mystery had become history.

The beings no longer looked within and without, finding their own essential connections, but only away from themselves, gazing ever upwards. Sometimes in looking up they were inspired to create great things. They built soaring spires and elegant domes, composed rousing choral pieces and painted exquisite devotional icons. And inevitably with the creative energy came compassion. Magnificent, selfless acts of kindness were inspired too. In the name of their God, or their creed, good was done.

Yet anything that kept the beings true nature hidden, even repressed, wasn't truly beneficial. Unquestioned tradition and worshipful devotion were diversions that fostered separation, keeping them from the Great Reunion.

The wild card had been played and those seeking spiritual control had won the hand...but not the game, surely? For an endless while it seemed so. The beings' ignorance of their Oneness allowed for the arrogant decimation of species, habitats and each other. Of course, despite the prevalent disconnection, there were always questing individuals that heeded their inner *knowing,* standing resolutely for unity. Some joined together in positive movements towards wholeness; others became trapped into different corners by belief. Yet the majority were mesmerised by a convenient lie; some deeply, others intermittently. Most were dulled by the influence that deliberately held back a mass awakening. Even when the threat of damnation receded the beings were so habituated to the separatist illusion that it seemed an unnecessary effort to look beyond it.

The nightmare of the forgetting *continued because it could.*

But even a recurring dream's cycle must find its end one day. Perhaps when the bad dream seemed at its worst the beings would awaken fully, shocked at last from their listless distractions.

The Wild Dreamer realised that every tide, no matter how vast or protracted its cycle, would become high again after a seemingly endless low and every wave would recede before breaking in sparkling droplets on the shore of consciousness. Perhaps now the waves would be that bit stronger, the push forward that much further...Yes, perhaps this time.

And so the process – that endless motion back to *forgetting* and forth towards *remembering* – continues. And while it does, amazing things are imagined, then made. Many beautiful, meaningful life-dreams are danced across the realms. Yet many suffer, struggle and inflict pain because of their continued separation from their collective Wild Self. To end this chapter of Our Creation Myth conclusively we need to reclaim our Creator-nature and awaken – *awaken now!* – to realise our Oneness. Not to worship it, nor become homogenised by it, but *be* it together; valuing every individual being as an equal expression of our Infinitely Conscious Self.

So, we can't state THE END here, or anywhere, until the Great Reunion has taken place – and perhaps not even then. For all is cyclical, in and out like a breath; round again like our apparent birth and death. All we can say is *this is where we are, in this particular shared Now.* This point could mark a whole new beginning for our contemporaries, for all beings we encounter; ever onwards, eternally unfolding.

Let it begin here, with us.

Clearly this story isn't an accurate chronicle. Nor is it a full and final statement. It's just a sweeping allegory to explain an energetic process; a way of understanding what we are and how we've ended up. It reveals the patterns and pitfalls inherent in existence and as such is an aid to living well, both for us and for all other beings.

Because our transformation is theirs.

What heals one heals All.

Leaving the Road to Nowhere

This book has no other agenda but to inspire our *remembering*.

As Our Creation Myth suggests, *remembering* is like 'coming to' after a particularly realistic nightmare. Once we've *remembered* our interconnectedness we can live more lovingly, with care for our other selves. In the next chapters I'll share practical methods by which we can do this.

But before we continue, let's address an old habit that's holding us all back.

The God habit.

The fundamental premise of wild spirituality is equality – a lasting empowerment based in our direct experience of who we are; human and non-human; seen and *unseen* beings alike. It offers a different basis for living harmoniously and completely, *with and for all our relations*. I say different as most defined spiritual paths see our Creator as being somehow *outside* us – a higher power – with all created beings viewed as distinct from us. No matter how well meaning it may be any spiritual way that perpetuates this perspective is part of the problem. Yes, our established traditions give people a way to pull focus on ethical behaviour. Yes, they give a sense of community responsibility and a soul-identity that's lacking in modern society. But ultimately they reinforce the 'us and them' and 'little me' paradigms that keep us from the wonder of our Self.

A Self that cannot be adequately expressed by an anthropomorphised Deity.

The vast majority of life-forms on Earth are non-human. We can't even begin to relate to the microscopic inhabitants of this land we live upon – or the oceans, or the sky above – let alone those realms or realities we'll never even guess at whilst incarnate! As we consider the probability of multiverses – layer upon layer of alternate universes in countless dimensions – the further we move from the human of Planet Earth. So why would any all-powerful Creator Deity be humanoid unless we'd created it in our image?

It's time to challenge our own ingrained human-centricity and expand our awareness of our Self.

After a lifetime of separation, embracing ourselves as Creator may seem the most appalling precocity. Yet such Self-aggrandisement is altogether positive. Just accepting we won't be punished for this apparently outrageous hubris is a significant step forward! Let's give our self permission to think we're absolutely wonder-full.

If we're the Oneness how can we not be?

So, there can be no God – or Goddess – in Our Creation Myth. As we'll discuss in Chapter Five, language is important and the words God and Deity will always have connotations of superiority and separateness...of 'out there-ness'. I may've used capitalisations to denote the Creator – using 'It' instead of 'it' etc. – but this is simply to express our Self as opposed to our self. The Wild Dreamer and the Wild Dream are just poetic terms to convey the all-encompassing essence we share. Infinite Consciousness and All Possibility express boundless, endless awareness without placing it anywhere, so limiting it.

We're All-That-Is; the witnessing eye of Infinite Consciousness and every little 'I' that has an experience. The One and the one – and everyone – simultaneously and instantaneously. There's nothing outside or above what we all are.

Access All Areas

In actuality we're beyond all labels; even those of 'individual', 'human' or 'spirit' which all pertain to the illusion of selfhood. As Jidda Krishnamurti said, *'when you call yourself a Christian, or a European, or anything else, you are being violent. When you separate yourself by belief, by nationality or tradition it breeds violence.'* Essentially we're not a something. Or an anything. *We're everything!* And *everything* can't be contained, explained, curtailed or set against itself.

We're beyond belief, as belief immediately boundaries perception and establishes a partition between believers and non-believers.

This isn't to say we shouldn't give meaning to, or have faith in, anything; nihilism being another diversion. But science with its need to prove, and religion with its need to accept, are opposite ends of the same stick. They're so involved with the details of their debate they fail to experience themselves 'outside the stick' where dynamic Creative Consciousness – everything including the stick – just is. Directly experiencing the free-flow of energy is the key; not adherence to, or wholesale rejection of, any one tenet.

To regress to any ideological comfort zone after coming to this understanding – this profound *remembering* – would be unsatisfying and exasperating unless we decide to deliberately deceive ourselves. As Krishnamurti also said, *'when you see something as false which you have accepted as true...then you can never go back to it.'* When we realise our Oneness – as hopefully we will through the inspiration in this book – then we can no longer cling to any comfortable pre-packaged philosophy.

It's time to ungild the spiritual lily and reveal the natural beauty. Truth is much simpler than the lie and it loves to go naked.

Just as the wind doesn't need to wear an overcoat, wild spirituality doesn't need to wear a disguise. It's as wilful as a badger following old tracks across man-made obstacles and as brisk as the east wind whipping across salt marshes. It has all the potency and delicacy of a wildflower left unpicked. It's a *living thing*, liberated from convention and bespoke, not off-the-peg. It's the guiding force of an autonomous, courageous being that knows itself as Itself.

This is, as the Tao so elegantly expresses it, a Way that's not a way: a pathless path.

A book about wild spirituality can only ever be an evocative guide, encouraging us to move into a sinuous spaciousness where everything's possible...and every being free to express its fullest potential.

Weighty Enlightenment

Please don't worry if this all seems a bit much now.

It's not the aim of this book to unsettle people so I suggest we just stay with the notion of Oneness for a while without dismissing or embracing it. If we open ourselves to a possibility then information and experiences will present themselves to support or refute our hypothesis. We'll give ourselves the clues that we need, as we need them.

For myself, I found that once I'd realised my – and our – true nature, it took me several years for the concept to permeate my psyche and touch my heart.

I went through three phases:

1. *I felt disorientated*: an anteater, a rosebush and a dictator couldn't all be the Creator surely? I wanted a Controller with a Grand Design, not a series of incompetents!
2. *I felt lost*: who could I pray to when I was in need? Who'd save me if I – and other fallible beings – were All-That-Is?
3. *I felt cheated*: surely I was a unique and significant individual, not just an illusory aspect of a Greater Self?

To realise – to *remember* – I was both *being and Being* was mind blowing and yet my mind didn't blow. I stuck with the discomfort of transformation and broke my addiction to the old self-ish paradigm one day at a time. Gradually Oneness became my new life focus. I abandoned any appellations I'd previously 'worn' for meaning – the Christian, the pagan, the spiritwalker –

and embraced the All (and the Nothing; the *no-thing*) I am. It's my hope this book will help you become all you are too. Gently and thoroughly.

Just take it moment by moment and let your awakening journey unfold as we travel into the green heart of being together.

CHAPTER TWO
Rewiring; Rewilding

'*To understand the immeasurable the mind must be extraordinarily quiet; still.*'

J. Krishnamurti'

'*If the doors of perception were cleansed then everything would appear to man as it is – infinite.*'

William Blake

'*It's just a choice – right here, right now – between fear and love.*

Bill Hicks

'*Foregoing self, the Universe grows 'I'.*'

Sir Edwin Arnold

This chapter begins the experiential part of the book. It'll enable us to empower and energise ourselves by re-accessing our Infinitely Conscious Self. The wild-spirited techniques that follow have been extensively tried-and-tested and can be used to safely connect to, and work with, the *unseen* for positive purposes.

All Will Be Revealed

Firstly let's clarify *unseen*. *Unseen* is italicised as it's a broad term, referring to any layer of existence, being or energy we don't generally witness with the five senses. The *unseen* is anything, and anyone, *beyond* – that is, outside our basic physical experience of 'ordinary reality'.

These include:

- Non-physical or energetic dimensions/levels/realms
- Inaccessible physical realms with different vibrational states/ frequencies to ours
- Human and non-human deceased; those currently disembodied or 'in spirit'
- Permanently disembodied, ethereal or energetic beings – not all aspects of awareness come into apparent manifest form
- Embodied/physical beings with different vibrational rates/ conditions to our own
- Our eternal Source-Self which is both enigmatic and fully present, because we are *It* made manifest.

The *unseen* isn't unreal, nor is it negligible. It shares our energetic space at all times, in all places, and is as authentic as this level of existence but is inaccessible by physical sight. It exists outside our limited spectrum of visible light and so isn't included in our 'consensus version' of reality...that which we know as 'ordinary reality'. Earthly species such as insects or birds can see light frequencies outside our visible spectrum but we're limited to the narrow band to the right of infrared and to the left of ultraviolet. In terms of wider energetic awareness we're virtually blind, confined within the tiny electro-magnetic range that our physical framework currently operates in. Although we may still experience with an 'extra-sensory' sixth sense, or deliberately look *beyond*, we're usually restricted to our body's immediate – and woefully inadequate – perceptions , believing what they reveal is all there is.

Respected mainstream scientists like Rolf-Dieter Heuer, Director of the Cern facility, acknowledge that we only understand four percent of this universe with the remaining ninety six percent labelled dark energy or matter. Given that our Creator-Self is endlessly creative – and that All Possibility is just that – we can hypothesise what exists in this hidden, but extant, energetic space...countless variations on the theme of reality; a myriad of expressions and levels of existence. These *unseen* aspects are deep within us, and every other being, just as they're in the furthest reaches of Creation Itself. We simply need to access them by different means than the usual – *psychically rather than physically.* But why?

We work with the *unseen* because:

1. It allows us to 'power up' by reconnecting to our Source-Self, thus becoming more effective and creative.
2. It enables us to commune with beneficent *unseen* mentors to gain beneficial insights or guidance that helps us live well... *for the good of the All.*
3. It broadens our horizons, making us more responsive and empathetic.

In this chapter we'll focus on the first issue, reconnecting to our Source-Self.

In the natural way of things we wouldn't need to do this as our 'hotline' would be fully, and effortlessly, functioning. But thanks to generations of imposed separation and fearful confusion – combined with the artificial environs most of us inhabit – it's likely the link we currently have is poor quality, with interference. By deliberately forging this link afresh, and strengthening it each day, we'll recharge, becoming stronger, gentler; *greater.* Decision making, relationships, health and creative direction will be enhanced by daily reconnection with our Source-Self.

But like all worthwhile things this takes effort on our part.

Routine Enquiries

Reconnection means *rewiring* ourselves to be recharged and earthed, allowing essential Source energy – the energy of Creation – to move safely through us and on. It also means *rewilding* ourselves – enlivening and enchanting our everyday lives by experiencing the ineffable. Once we do this, all else follows. In fact, our life *flows* better than before because we're more aware of the energy that fuels and forms it.

Yet it's worth mentioning that we may not find this routine reconnection easy. In fact we may find we make excuses not to engage regularly, perhaps because we feel it'd be worse to fail connecting than not to try at all. Even though it may seem daunting, the more we do it the more natural and worthwhile it becomes; which is why reconnection through meditation is referred to as a *practice*.

And there's no way we can fail to connect with our Greater Selves: we're already One! We just need to get reacquainted.

Reconnecting isn't about *doing* anything, as such. We don't have to strive just as we don't have to force our heart to beat or deliberately breathe when we're asleep. Such activity is as instinctive – or as programmed – as the germination of a seed in the warming earth. Similarly a computer appears to be doing nothing when it's downloading information and a laptop recharges from the mains supply without seeming actively occupied. Recharging, or downloading, appear as passive processes yet their stillness conceals engagement. Likewise our reconnection requires *focussed acquiescence,* not exertion.

Let's continue with the laptop analogy. We wouldn't expect it, or any other gadget, to run continuously without a top up to its battery, or with coffee spilled over it. So it us with us humans, we need regular and safe top ups. Not just physically but spiritually or *energetically.* Yes, we've functioned thus far without intentionally recharging (although we've certainly 'plugged in' unconsciously), but we'll be more effective when we do it deliberately. All the natural power – the wild energy – of our Source-Self is available free, at all times, to make us the most potent, vivid version of ourselves we can be.

If we're to function optimally, reconnection needs to become a good habit.

And how much time a day does this habit require? That's entirely up to us and is something we'll discover from experience. As a guide to begin with, let's say the time it takes to comfortably eat breakfast; approximately twenty minutes. Of course we can consume our tea and toast in less time and give our connection less time too. But if we're to get the best out of the experience then setting aside twenty minutes is perfectly adequate. Our reconnection is as essential as breakfast and equally important in setting us up for the day. Plus it's best engaged in before we're 'on the go'; when we're still fresh and unlikely to be distracted or fall asleep. In return for getting up a little earlier to set aside the quiet time, we gain an inner strength for our daily interactions.

Of course, we can 'plug in' again in the evening. We'll also find that as we put our wild-spirited ideas into practice, our very existence will become an act of fully-conscious connection. But a deliberate recharging first thing is a statement of intent and an act of self-empowerment, centring us in what's important. It gives us clarity and vitality, therefore we put it before all else. It's *primary*.

But how best to do it? I'd suggest *carefully*.

Safety First

Safe reconnection means consciously aiming above the lower *unseen* levels. Low here means close or heavy – the energetic realms nearest to our own dense reality.

These levels hold an imprint of our energetic outpourings; our thoughts and imaginings. Although humanity creates great beauty and feels immense love, our separation from our selves – and our Self – means there's also a constant outpouring of fear. Fear is the *forgetting;* love the *remembering.* All fearful actions such as war or abuse feed hostile, angry, distressed emanations into the energetic, or *etheric,* realms. What we do here has a resonance there. We're all creators and our 'invisible' thoughts have power to effect change in more worlds than this. If fear-driven emotions or ideas are dwelled on with sufficient force or regularity then energetic forms are created in the ether. We need to be aware of what we, and others, put out as our predominant signal.

Everything is energy and our energies are everything.

Secondly, because Creation encompasses every imaginable aspect, there are many *unseen* beings and energies that're not beneficial to us. They range from the inherently mischievous to the downright malevolent, along with those that cause harm unintentionally by their sheer incompatibility. Some beings are vampiric and live off of the energy of others, like a dragonfly lava feeds off its unwitting host. Others seek clinging symbiosis, like ivy growing on an oak. Still others seem to relish hurting us, like a wasp stinging gratuitously at the end of its season. Some are unconcerned with us yet naturally feed on our waste, like a fly on a cowpat. Some are harmless yet bother us by their very being, like a spider in our bathtub. And like a lion bringing down a zebra, others can't help but prey on us because *that's what they do.* For every physical aspect of Creation there's an *unseen* equivalent somewhere, so for every charming squirrel there's bound to be a scorpion or flea.

Let's look at this from a different angle. Just as our Source-Self encompasses all aspects of Creation, including the disagreeable ones, there're envious, callous, vicious parts of our individual selves. We know we're capable of unpleasant behaviours but we choose to keep them in check. What's in us at a small, personal level is in us at an expansive, communal level. And vice versa. When we understand this we can be as fair, but resolutely firm, to challenging beings as we are to our own – and hopefully others' – shortcomings.

If we behave cautiously, but not fearfully when we approach the *unseen,* then we're prepared. This isn't being negative or neurotic but as sensible as recognising venomous arachnids if we visit Australia. My advice for reconnecting has protection at its strong core so we never have to waste time dealing with troublesome energies. With an understanding of what exists *beyond* we're more likely to keep our practice disciplined and aimed at the highest possible good. If we focus our endeavours at the most sublime expression of our Source-Self then we're unlikely to flounder.

Even if we already have our own experience of tuning into the subtle realms we can all benefit from a refresher course as it's easy to become jaded, blasé and lax. What I suggest is a threefold approach that begins with protection, focuses on our breath then *enters the silence* of profound, refreshing connection.

Before we do any of this we need consider our physical position and be sitting – or lying – both comfortably and appropriately.

Back to Our Roots

Our physical position assists reconnection. As wild spirituality is centred on the green heart of being I've chosen the tree as our model.

As most ancient cultures concurred, the tree is an eloquent symbol of the connection between earth and sky; that which is simultaneously grounded and open. By aligning ourselves with the primal Tree of Life, or World Tree, we take on its powerful resonance and use our own body as a similar bridge, becoming as 'living wood'. Our spine-trunk becomes the metaphorical wire through which we conjoin both our physical and eternal aspects; allowing the pure pulse of Source energy to move through us just as a tree draws in sunlight and water. We all know how something as familiar, but wonderful, as a tree functions and so can emulate them easily.

Our intent is consistently vital and if we intend to be as a tree, imagining ourselves as they are, then it'll be so. After all, we're the Creator and dreaming-into-being is our forte.

Now we need to get into a position that allows for firm contact with the earth whilst suggesting openness to what lies beyond us. Although trees stand upright, standing isn't practical for deep relaxation over twenty minutes. Instead we can sit or lie down whilst maintaining the basic principle of *tree-ness,* with our spine as conduit-trunk. The spine itself lengthens into a tap root that gives stability whilst smaller roots branch off other parts. If we're sitting it can look like this:

If we're lying like this:

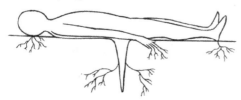

I don't assume one physical *modus operandi* for all and suggest we use whatever position we've previously found comfortable for meditation/contemplation and *root ourselves deep into it.* We're presenting ourselves *symbolically* and so with a little ingenuity we can adapt our most comfortable posture into representing a tree's essential grounded openness.

The position of our limbs/hands/feet is also important. The diagrams below offer some suggestions:

1. When our body's 'wires' are uncrossed – our legs and arms unbent or unfolded – we can allow for an unimpeded flow of energy.

2. When we sit in the classic yogic position of the sages, an effective circuit is created.

3. When the soles of our feet and our palms are touching we make another functioning circuit.

4. When we place the palms and the soles of the feet flat on the ground we earth ourselves, allowing energy to pass though us and onwards.

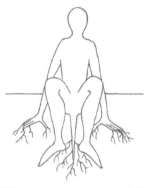

5. When our palms and feet face upwards we show receptivity to All-That-Is.

All these postures are equally effective so we can choose what feels right, physically and symbolically. There's no right and wrong with wild spirituality, only a need to understand our choices.

Bubbling Up

Now we're positioned we can use our imagination and intent to protect ourselves.

In wild spirituality, intention is everything. In this case, if we deliberately and passionately focus on what we want – to be protected from harmful energies – then it'll be so. What we give our full attention to through visualisation – seeing with our mind's eye – becomes reality at an energetic or *unseen* level. Yet protection isn't absolutely infallible. By this I mean if we deliberately venture into disturbed atmospheres or seek out hostile forces then we can expect repercussions. After all, if we keep our hand on a hot stove an oven glove will only keep us from burning for so long. However, if we only give our attention to what's benevolent and uplifting, not dangerously disconcerting, then the following protective process will be more than enough.

After years of experimentation I've found visualising a bright protective bubble the most effective method. This visualisation can be backed up by describing what's being created, either aloud or internally. *Stating our intent* is a powerful adjunct to inner work, with invocation or affirmation being a partner to visualisation. It's particularly effective if we need protection fast. If our protective routine is well established then a few evocative words like '*I'm safe in my shining bubble*' will be enough to trigger it into being.

The first protective bubble I'll describe is suitable for daily use. It's made of an etheric gel, inspired by the translucent gelatine-free capsule my vitamins come in. These capsules are strong enough to hold powder yet flexible enough to be squashed without breaking. They're also insubstantial enough to melt in the mouth. I find this combination of subtlety and strength perfect for the protective material I need to visualise.

With my inner vision I see myself standing inside a protective semi-transparent membrane which is tinted a bright sky blue. I see this above my head and below my feet; before and behind me and to both sides, surrounding me from top to toe. I reach out and test this 'second skin', feeling it give a little under my fingers. I mentally describe what I'm experiencing ('*I'm standing within a bright blue gel bubble...*' etc.) to strengthen its reality. Then I visualise the bubble filling with dazzling light, shielding

47

my eyes from its brilliance. I imagine how this must look from the outside; a glowing blue-white sphere in space. Then I allow the light to fade and I remain inside my capsule, knowing my intention has made it powerfully shielding yet not rigid or brittle. It flexes as I breathe – it's *organic*.

If I choose I can then shrink my bubble down so it covers me like an etheric space suit. I'm literally wrapped within its flexible fabric from head to toe. I look through the pale sky-coloured material in front of my face and 'see' myself wiggling fingers and toes through its fine translucent skin. As I begin my work I gradually lose a sense of wearing this blue suit or bubble, although it remains an energetic reality. The more times I create it the stronger its reality.

My second protective bubble is for ad-hoc use when I need swift, extra-strong protection. This could be in an unexpectedly hostile situation, with confrontational physical influences or disturbed *unseen* energies. This bubble's made of an 'alien' or otherworldly material – a preternaturally light, but incredibley resilient, super-metal. This shining metal has 'memory' so that if the bubble were dented it'd return to its original spherical shape. It's not so dense as to be impermeable but not so insubstantial as to be easily breached. It reflects light – and anything else directed at it – from its surface like a mirror and I fill it with light on the inside. Being in this bubble is like being inside a hollow ball-bearing...only one made from a gossamer-fine, strangely flexible but durable metal as yet unknown to humanity. This bubble can also be shrunk to fit into a flexible silver bodysuit.

I then stand ready within my protective sphere or suit, knowing it to be effective. If I've given my creation my full concentration and it feels convincing to me then I'll have the faith to project my protection psychically. Everything in the *unseen* is about energies and if we believe our protection to be real then it's an energetic reality.

Everything is energy and our energies are everything.

However, if I so choose I can now add a protective symbol over my body as a finishing touch.

Metaphorically Speaking

Symbols are potent shorthand representing a personal, or collective, concept. They're lyrical, expressive and compelling, resonating deeply at the super-conscious, or infinitely conscious, level. They may have been claimed by human belief systems but are beyond literal interpretation and belong to no one.

We can 'wear' any vibrant symbol that seems positively protective to us. Usually I choose a five-pointed silver star. I imagine it so that the upper point of it is above my head, the arms are my arms outstretched and two lower points are my legs apart. I imagine that the silver is burnished until it gleams and glints. I visualise it getting brighter, then let its light be absorbed into my outstretched body. I realise that this five pointed symbol has connotations of the pentacle, or witchcraft, but my choice is a star because it represents incandescent illumination in the darkness. I'm drawn to the star's eternal wild-spirited resonance, not its limited human interpretation.

However, this isn't to say we can't choose a symbol that's been charged up by specific focus or faith, such as the Om, Star of David, Yin-Yang, or Ankh. An equal armed cross, like the Celtic cross or medicine wheel, works well with a human body standing arms outstretched and legs together. It is of course a plus-sign (+) and so has positive associations.

As with my star we can place one large symbol over our whole self. Or we can position smaller versions over specific areas. If we work with the notion of chakras – energy points or portals on the body – then these would be ideal places to envision them.

Obviously we can also invent our own symbols. One I've worked with extensively represents the wild spirit:

49

To me, this combines the unfolding of All Possibility (spiral) supporting the wild dream of the Earth (curve) holding each individual being (dot) which then feeds back into the spaciousness of Infinite Consciousness (all around it and back to the spiral's centre). It speaks of the eternal flow of One to one to One again. It also looks like a joyous individual with their arms raised and a wild spiral of spirit fuelling them. To you it may mean something else entirely, and that's how it should be. Please feel free to utilise it! But with the wild-spirited do-it-yourself ethos it'd be better to meditate on Oneness, then create your own.

Breathing Space

Now we're positioned and protected it's time to focus on our breath.

Why is focussing on the breath such a central tenet of meditation practice across philosophies? Because breath is the great leveller; no incarnate creature is above or beyond it, regardless of any perceived divisions. Trying to resist the urge to breathe is futile. It's such an innate feature of existence that we do it automatically...*like now as we read these words*. But as we've probably just noticed, our automatic breathing is generally shallow and unsatisfactory.

Previously we may've only noticed our breathing when we were nervous and needed to calm ourselves. Then we deliberately take deep slow breaths. We need to amend this so that we become aware of our breathing regularly, monitoring it throughout our day. This is called *being with the breath*: staying focussed in awareness of inhalation and exhalation. Being with the breath is intimate and immediate, being accessible to us at all times.

By this we'll become *deeper awake*: maintaining an alert presence rather than being a somnambulist who assumes they're fully conscious. This deep awake/aware state makes us more lucid in our life-dream, allowing us to affect positive change more readily. We become less reactionary (operating from the base level of human emotions and the fight-or-flight mechanism) and more *response*-able (capable of considered behaviour centred in our eternal nature).

We'll look at practical means by which we can live lucidly in Part Two. For now let's begin our new era of enhanced consciousness by centring on our breath.

To begin, let's move our hand to our diaphragm as to feel what's happening deep within us. Feel the rise and fall of our chest as oxygen is taken in and carbon dioxide released. Listen to the sound the air makes as it's inhaled and exhaled. Make each breath deeper and slower; more deliberate. There's nothing more important than this moment, this breath. In and out, rising and falling, holding and releasing again. Our breath is nebulous – seemingly insubstantial – yet it makes our material body respond tangibly and energises it. Our breath is miraculous and yet utterly mundane. In and out, rising and falling, holding and releasing.

This simple act helps if we've become detached from our bodily processes. Yet we're also realising that *we're not our bodies* and so identifying with it completely would be a regressive move. Denying the body negates our current individual experience while neglecting our eternal aspect renders the experience meaningless. It's a case of holding the balance – having a more intimate connection with our apparent physicality (the seen aspect) even as we know it's not who we truly are (Infinite Consciousness; the *unseen* aspect).

This is dual awareness.

Focussing on the breath reveals how connected both aspects are, making us aware of our totality; our oneness...and so the Oneness of all things.

Now, as we sit or lie in our position we can use our breath to reconnect. This we do through a process called *entering the silence*.

The Sound of Silence

We enter the silence by being with our breath and deliberately ceasing the litany of internal chatter that marks our lives. When we still our unquiet human mind we immediately dissolve the boundaries between big/small, inner/outer, physical/non-physical because when our temporary self is quiet *all there is is what we are*: our Source-Self. When we *enter the silence* we're in a state of *mindless mindfulness*; simply being, not doing. We're in a place of no-place, between all worlds yet a part of all of them.

We just are.

This sounds impossibly esoteric or tricksy until we engage in the process. It's rather like riding a bike or driving a car; when faced with the mechanics of what's involved it seems too complicated. We think we'll never get from stationary to a being out on our own, enjoying the journey. Still, if we keep practicing, we find – like magic – that one day we're actually riding/driving without effort. And before too long we're able to have a conversation or sing along to music while we're doing it; it's become second nature to us. If we were asked to keep five batons in the air simultaneously after reading a manual called 'How to Juggle' we'd know it wasn't possible, except by a fluke. Similarly no amount of description can help us *enter the silence*. We need to begin it now. But how?

1. *We focus on the breath; only on the breath.* We inhale deeply through our nostrils, and hold for a count of three, and then exhale through the mouth. The sound we make is like the sea: on the in breath the tide pulls back and then there's a moment of stasis when the quiet wave is suspended before being released onto the shore with a rush. *In and out.* This is a soothing sound; the rhythm of life on this planet. It's the sibilant hiss of All-That-Is as it contracts and expands again

after countless, unfathomable aeons. It's the comforting yet powerful pulse of all Creation. And on we breathe – *in and out; deeper and slower* – merging with the wild ocean of existence and acceptance.

2. *This whisper and whoosh of breath is the only noise we're aware of now.* All other sounds die back as if the volume of everyday life is being turned down. We're only tuned into that lulling sea-sound of breathing. *In and out; deeper and deeper.* Becoming ever less vigilant but more sentient.

3. *We let any extraneous thoughts rise up and dissolve like sea mist in the midday sun.* We observe them without engaging with their meaning. Those musings belong to our temporary human persona and not to our Source-Self. Our Self can observe them as illusions within the life-dream, nothing more. They become more insubstantial with each breath as we breathe deeply, slowly and evenly. *In and out.* With each breath we free ourselves from any trivial desires that tether us, keeping us tame.

4. *We let any troublesome residual feelings go.* In this timeless time – this perpetual *Now* – they aren't relevant. They don't own us, we don't own them. We don't push them forcibly away, but witness them like driftwood bobbing by on an ocean of awareness before letting them disappear. We simply breathe. *In and out.* We're flowing without moving.

5. *We keep focussing on our breath; only on the breath.* Everything temporary and human is dissolving except the breath; that alone keeps us in touch with our temporal existence. We're All Possibility relaxing into ever-expanding eternity. We're Infinite Awareness allowing the experience to unfold. *In and out.* There's nothing else but this moment. We're All. All is well. *All is.*

6. *We gently bring our attention back to our breath of our singular body.* We let the sensations of our body become known once more; greeting them as friends. We allow this reality to filter

back in. We begin to hear the sounds and scents of the place we're in. Our awareness is back with our individual perspective in the life-dream. We're Infinite Consciousness experiencing existence through the filter we currently call 'me'.

7. *We return fully to 'ordinary reality'.* We aim to keep an awareness of our breath as we move through our day.

How Was It for You?

What can we expect to happen when we *enter the silence*? Well, everything and nothing! There's no way to describe an experience beyond words. We're all individual points of perception and each encounter will reflect that. I can only give you a flavour of how it is for me and that isn't for a right or wrong comparison but just to share.

I find that once I'm deeply relaxed and centred on my breath I can flick my dual awareness like a switch. I deliberately move it from my singular small self to that of the Source-Self. I'm not seeking, just aiming my attention at that level of being. It's always there; I'm just focussing on it.

As soon as I do this I'm in the *dazzling darkness*. My human eyes are closed and I'm in absolute blackness but I'm also at the heart of the wildfire of Creation. A brilliance beyond earthly illumination envelopes me. With the coming of this incredible light – the same light that was originally created to contrast with the fertile void – my head tilts back as if pulled and Source energy pours through me. It tingles deliciously in my extremities, making me buzz. Sometimes I weep softly and I often laugh, overcome with the wordless understanding of my *remembering*; engulfed yet absolutely calm. As if I was parched I drink in the Great Mystery that's me: *that's us*. I bathe in it, refreshing my entire being. Yet nothing happens. I don't do anything at all. It's just in me and I am in it, serene and accepting.

I rise above my petty self, and all my foibles, without going anywhere. It's like dying without being born.

I could so easily be absorbed back into the endless kind-light and be free again. But every time, I chose to come back to my human self, grateful for being able to experience All-That-Is from a particular point of perception.

That's the best I can do to explain what it's like for me. But for you?

You and I are All Possibility. Therefore anything is possible.

There could be curiously familiar and tantalising intimations on the edge of our awareness. We may feel as if we're blissfully moving through space even as we know we're stationary; travelling without leaving. Or we may remain in a state of absolute tranquillity, floating in endless bliss.

Who knows. Or rather, who dares to dream. All that can be said categorically is whatever we experience is what we are. Because we're everything.

All we're doing is reminding ourselves of that fact.

Personal Effects

Although what we witness when we *enter the silence* may seem compelling it's not really important. Any 'pyrotechnics and phenomena' are just that – attractive distractions. They're a bit of imaginative fun, not the whole point. They're just transient transmissions from our infinitely inspired Creator-Self...the one that just can't help but ask '*what if?*' to see what happens. It's just us – the bigger Us – playing with possibilities.

If we think of the things we experience as pulses from an incredibly distant star – fascinating in themselves but not pertinent to our current life – then we can witness them with 'disinterested interest'. If we think we're more 'spiritually advanced' because we've 'bells and whistles' in our meditative practice – or indeed in any of our wild-spirited work – then we're allowing ourselves to get sidetracked. Any amazement should be a phase, not the permanent condition. Let any phenomena arise, witness them, then let them go.

We may argue *'but what I experience seems so meaningful; so personal! Surely I should pay attention?'* to which I'd respond *'everything seems personal to us because we're everything'*. When we 'touch base' with our Self after a long absence we're bound to feel overwhelmed and emotional. It's a beautiful reunion, after all – one with a long lost relative we only just found we had, and who turns out to be more our self than we are. We're all that has ever been or will ever be, and to reconnect with this glorious wild power is a marvellous thing. It creates marvels!

And what is the *Now*? It's just the Witness and the witnessed, together in the eternal moment.

Everything else – time, space, individuality, every created thing – is illusory: a perfect, valid – and yet entirely evanescent – figment of Our imagination.

By *entering the silence* we're in that perfect crux point of stillness from which all things proceed and to which all things return. We're in that pause between inhalation *(being)* and exhalation *(nothingness)* where the *Is* and *Is Not* co-exist; the place of All Potentiality. The author Dr. Wayne W. Dyer calls this *getting into the gap*.

It's a real homecoming.

And like any home it restores us, reminds us of who we are and makes us feel loved unconditionally. The more we go there the better we feel. It's not what happens when we're there but the going itself that counts. Even if we just 'pop in' every day, we get the benefit. And so does every other being, whether we meet them or not.

Ground Control

Again this may seem like a lot to take in at first but soon the routine will seem completely normal to us.

As a tool for remembering, it reads:

- *Positioning*
- *Protecting*
- *Breathing*

- *Entering*
- *Returning*
- *Grounding*

We'll notice that we haven't covered *grounding* yet. This means to ground ourselves in our apparent physicality – in 'ordinary reality' – so we can adequately focus on the rest of our day.

I suggest:

- *Clapping* the hands, clicking the fingers, stamping the feet
- *Stretching* as luxuriantly a cat does on awakening
- *Feeling* the texture of clothing, floor, hair, skin
- *Scenting* the air or an essential oil/herb placed nearby for the purpose
- *Eating* a biscuit or cracker, sucking a piece of fruit, drinking water or juice

More ways of grounding ourselves by paying attention to manifest reality are suggested in Chapter Six.

Before we move on to the next chapter it's worth mentioning that the more we *enter the silence* the more our notion of what's real can begin to shift...with surprising results.

Synchronised Swimming with the Cosmic Tide

There're as many realities as there are possibilities; that is to say *an infinite number.*

It makes me smile that scientists come up with a precise number of universes – multiverses – based on a 'provable theory'. To suggest that All Possibility would stop creating at one version, eleven versions or even seventy three versions is rather preposterous. If we look to our Earth for clues we could consider how many variations on a beetle there are. Certainly there are lots, although not an unlimited variety. But then how many more could there be elsewhere, in other worlds? In other dimensions? And how many in potentiality, as yet unmanifest?

All Possibility has no loopholes or caveats. It just is, endlessly.

Unlimited versions of reality – including this one – just are.

When we reconnect, we'll find our Creator Self will start creating in all sorts of unexpected ways. And so I'd like to offer a light-hearted caution here.

Once we begin to push the boundaries of our existence we may begin to notice the warp and the weft of the fabric of our own lives going a little wonky.

The main way we can observe this is in the frequency of what we call *synchronicities*; that is, incredible coincidences. As with so many words we use to describe the ineffable – like 'spirit' and 'spirituality' – 'synchronicity' and 'coincidence' sound clichéd and clunky. But they're all we have so I hope I can be excused for using them.

Here's a typical sample of my synchronicitous events. A glass smashed in my kitchen, at the same time the presenter on my radio said '*a glass smashed in my kitchen*'. Fair enough! But a week later exactly the same thing happened, just as the narrator of my audio book said '*the glass shattered*'. Recently I was admiring the thick dark hair of a Japanese man. I observed to my friend that Asian people were fortunate not to go bald as often as Caucasians. My friend said women were also lucky as he'd never seen a balding woman. Moments later a near-bald Chinese lady walked directly past us. It was as if we'd conjured her up to prove ourselves wrong. Or perhaps she'd conjured us to illustrate a point of her own! This week I was going for an MRI scan. I had the radio on before I left the house. As I mentally berated myself for not researching the safety implications beforehand the radio presenter suddenly stated '*it's known that MRI's are perfectly safe*'. Why, thank you!

Similar occurrences happen to me every day, sometimes in such rapid succession as to be absurd. I believe this is because my questing, wild-spirited practice is constantly tuning me back into the expansiveness of *What Is* instead of the false construct we've been presented with, and somehow agreed to, as our 'consensus reality'. I call this attunement being *on the One* – staying with the pulse rather than flailing behind the true beat. When I'm *on the One* I'm open to 'the web of wyrd' (or *weird*) and so the experiences are fascinating but not that surprising or bizarre. Synchronicities reveal that the fabric of existence is more supple, diaphanous and *intelligent* than we've previously experienced it to be. Life is meant to be an ongoing interactive experience, with creation happening spontaneously and instantaneously. It's being shut down and inured in a limited world that's strange!

Because interactive creativity is our true state, we shouldn't get too involved in the hidden meaning of our synchronicities. That way lies superstition, even a loss of sanity. It's what's behind the coincidences – the reminder of our true Creator-nature – that matters. If we maintain our receptiveness to *What Is* we can do, see or be anything within – and perhaps outside – the realms of possibility. We can consciously co-create as we were meant to, responding to that eternal wild impetus of '*what if?*'.

If we allow ourselves to receive what our Infinitely Conscious Self can reveal to us, gently pushing back the confines of awareness, then who knows what we can understand or achieve.

All we need is to reconnect, be receptive and see what happens... without fear.

CHAPTER THREE
Seeking Sanctuary

'When blackthorn petals pearl the breeze, there are the twisted hawthorn trees,
Thickset with buds, as clear and pale, as golden water or green hail –
As if a storm of rain had stood, enchanted in the thorny wood,
And hearing fairy voices call, hung poised, forgetting how to fall.'

Mary Webb

'With things that are rooted, and firm, and deep,
Quiet to lie, and dreamless to sleep;
With things that are chainless, and tameless, and proud,
With the fire in the jagged thundercloud...'

Dora Greenwell

'Though we travel the world over to find the beautiful
We must carry it with us or we find it not'.

Ralph Waldo Emerson

In the last chapter we reconnected with our Source, or Creator, Self. This chapter is about exercising our creative aspect to work with energies, and so shape reality, for positive purposes.

What follows is a guide to creating an etheric sanctuary; an *unseen* wild haven we can visit at any time for replenishment and fresh insights. In the next chapter we'll learn about the benevolent beings – our *unseen* companions or guides – that we can invite into this sanctuary; discovering who they are, how we meet them and why. As we're in an (apparently) physical dimension, and our prospective companions are at an *unseen* level, we'll need to imagine/create a place 'between the worlds' – an otherworldly space where we can meet. Here we'll set up this safe space, both as a place of personal contemplation and for any potential trysts.

Wild at Heart

What we'll be envisioning, and so creating, will be a wild home from home. Not the kind of idyllic, bucolic residence that has four walls, but rather a wildwood lair: the Robin Hood-style refuge that we may dream of for our wilder, bolder self.

A special place in the deep green heart of being.

We'll mention the deep green heart continually in this book. Here it'll take form and become a lair in the primal forest – the untamed, verdant, mysterious place we all yearn for but which is all but lost to our world. But the green heart is also *allegorical*, symbolising the unconditional generosity that the trees have, both in sustaining our existence on Earth and providing shelter/sustenance for creatures. The greenness expresses freshness, tenderness and naiveté in the purest, simplest sense...all desirable qualities. It also symbolises eco-awareness, placing value on the natural and organic. The heart represents the compassion that sparks an ardent need for truth and justice. Together they exemplify the essential empathetic impetus that pulses at the hub of a life lived well...*for the good of the All.*

It's no coincidence that in Hindu and Buddhist traditions the heart chakra – or core energy centre – is coloured green. Its intense beat unites us in loving acceptance, thrumming with the same unreserved animating force that makes universes expand and contract.

We're all of the One Heart – a deeply green and wild heart.

Any journey to this heart of being will of course be a return journey to the centre of our Wild Self. We've begun to make this outward – yet inward and ultimately homeward – journey in our daily reconnection. Here I'm suggesting another way of experiencing reunion, this time utilising our innate creative skills to bring the deep green heart to life. We'll create a place of refuge and inspiration that'll facilitate a relationship with both our true nature and our spiritual allies. Then we'll journey there.

But how?

Trance Formation

By making a journey I mean a *trance journey*. We'll utilise these frequently in our wild-spirited work.

A trance isn't an out-of-control state in which we get manipulated or duped. It's a deeply relaxed, receptive state in which we're able to look *beyond* 'ordinary reality'. We use trance when we *enter the silence* only on a journey we go further; deeper in. A trance journey is an *inner* journey that travels without leaving; bypassing the critical intellect of the human self and moving into the realms of the imaginative eternal self. These are the same responsive realms – that same fertile energetic expansiveness – that our Wild Dreaming Self creates in. The reality we create in this malleable ether will be authentic; ethe*real*. The only difference between it and the physical place we're currently in is that it'll be at a subtler level of existence, indiscernible to the five senses.

However, we'll respond as though it is discernible. It'll be an immediate and compelling experience.

Just as for a manifest journey, we'll follow a prescribed route for a specific purpose, beginning with our safe routine for *entering the silence* and then looking *beyond* to envision and create. As a guideline I'll share a template inner journey here. It'll take us to a version of a wildwood lair I've created and act as a springboard for our own ideas. It's included so we can become acquainted with the procedure, not to be strictly adhered to. Please use it as a framework, keeping to the same basic structure, and then let your own imagination soar.

As you read through my journey keep these points in mind, then utilise them in your own version:

1. *A journey should have an outward bound section, an arrival/ working section and a return.* The route has to be followed as if it were actually happening. We can't just appear at our sanctuary then somehow get back without going to and from. The journey itself is an important part of the trance process and shortcuts won't help.

2. *A wild journey is in-the-round or cyclical,* as is nature's way.

3. *It should contain each element – earth, air, fire, water (ether* is the fifth; the *unseen* energy that combines them all) – making a unified environment.

4. *Our 'inner senses' should all be employed to make our encounter convincing.* We should touch, taste, see and smell as well as monitoring how we feel along the way.

5. *Our journey doesn't need stark modernity.* We're in a *time-out-of-time* and any associations with the contemporary or manmade will be distracting and jarring. Think wholesome, unpretentious and uncontrived.

6. *The number three helps create a magical place.* Three is a potent feature in folklore – three wishes/kisses/siblings/kings, the holy trinity. Because the magical power of three – *one two, three!* – is embedded in our psyche it takes us deeper *beyond* effortlessly. In my journey we'll have three barriers to overcome and we'll cross to *the other side* by three stepping stones.

7. *Finding a way through the forest is a powerful metaphor for discovering hidden truth,* or our authentic nature. However, the journey to our wild lair can be in any other untamed setting. But how to journey at all?

Follow Your Heart – Journey to the Centre of Yourself

We'll begin this, and any other, inner journey by going through the protective process to *enter the silence.* The only difference is that when we've *entered the silence,* we don't come straight back and ground ourselves. Instead we breathe deeper and slower, deeper and slower, focussing on the darkness behind our closed eyes.

We look at this as if we're looking at a cinema screen onto which we can project anything we like.

The screen's blank and dark. Yet perhaps now in the centre there's a flicker of light. Yes, it's growing, imperceptibly at first but now...

From the dazzling darkness of All Potentiality a vision forms, expanding to fill our awareness.

It's of a simple track; a flattened trail leading away through tall grass into the trees that stand to the north. As we watch, the grass ripples and the bright wildflowers nod. It's early morning, for the sun is still low, yet there's warmth – the promise of a glorious day ahead. A fat bumblebee zigzags past. We feel the urge to step onto that grassy track, feeling the dew beneath our bare feet and so step forward into that scene...

We go into the glistening green.

Looking down we see our feet in the grass and feel its damp coolness. We wiggle our toes then take another step on the subtly defined trail. Then we slowly bring our attention up, noting what we're wearing on our legs. It may not be the same thing we were wearing a minute ago, back in 'ordinary reality'. Now we take our attention to our hands, lifting them up to be examined. Perhaps they look the same as they do usually, perhaps not. We spend a moment flexing the fingers, studying the palms. We notice any jewellery we're wearing, or not.

We reacquaint ourselves with our wild self.

Then we take our gaze up and lift our head to the sky. It's a brilliant blue, punctuated by puffs of white cloud. There's a light warm breeze that's moving them along and ruffling our clothes. As we look up a lark rises, higher and higher, piping its singular trilling melodies. Its magical song remains clear even as it disappears from view.

We then bring our attention back to what lies before us and get drawn further into the scene.

We begin to move carefully towards the trees. These deciduous species, native to our own land, form a wood that stretches in either direction. The track on which we walk gets more pronounced as we approach. By the time we've reached the wood's outskirts we're following a path, marked by the paws and claws of passing creatures. It leads us to the threshold between sunlit open country and dappled shade, winding off into the leafy interior before us.

We pause, breathe deeply and listen.

Within the wood we hear the leaves of beech, ash and hazel whispering in their ancient, labyrinthine tongue. There's a rustling in the leaf litter as a shrew scurries from our tread. A blackbird's warning call punctuates the stillness. Immediately aware of being watched we freeze, scanning the deep green ahead. And there beside a young oak stands a doe with her large liquid eyes wide. As we hold our position, and our breath, a squirrel darts across a nearby branch chattering shrilly. Surprised, we step back and when we look again the doe has slipped away.

As we go on the temperature falls slightly and the texture of the path beneath our feet changes. Now the earth is dry and gritty and we tread on layers of beech mast, broken fir cones and bits of twig. Each step on this path takes us further from humanity's interventions and into an untamed verdant realm. As we step into the wood we speak softly:

'*With honour to all who grow and dwell here, I walk in peace, for peace. As within; so without.*'

We touch our heart, our forehead and our lips to indicate that we feel love, seek wisdom and speak true with a gentle spirit. Then we bow low to this living land and say:

'*May the unseen beings who come for my highest good accompany me now, even if I do not know them yet.*'

Then we move off, deeper into the green.

The path takes us first past a stand of silver birch whose leaves sound like rain as they stir in the breeze. We feel the texture of their papery bark peeling back from their slim trunks. A tiny iridescent beetle makes its way across and disappears under a loose curl of bark. Above us we hear a jay give its strident call. We move past beech trees, the knots in their greyish elephant-skin bark appearing as eyes that watch us solemnly. As we pass we touch velvety baby hazel leaves and the glossy emerald prickles of a holly bush. Further on we crouch down and turn an old log, witnessing the teeming life secreted beneath. Down there, under the dense leaf canopy where the sun barely penetrates, we smell sweet rot and damp loam.

Touching the earth we hold the woodland air within us. We're connected to this place. All is well.

Continuing on we find a bank to one side of our path. As we get nearer we see it's peppered with holes, with freshly excavated earth and small pale stones scattered beneath. We lean close, listening for the movement of mammals within. We imagine badgers curled up safe together, waiting for twilight. But there's only the sound of our heartbeat and a distant woodpecker tapping. Our hands touch the springy jewel-bright mosses, caressing the tiny fronds of viridian and gold. We brush the unfurling ferns with our fingers. Then we see behind the burrow-laden bank to the lavender mist beyond. Fortunately our path veers to the left and enters this glade, the carpet of bluebells emitting a subtle floral perfume that compliments the earthy spice of the wood. We marvel at the bluebells' delicately fluted, nodding caps and the thrusting green blades of their shoots; the beauty in both their fragility and their boldness.

A pheasant hears us coming now and gives his throaty alarm call. When his sound has died down there's only the padding of our own bare feet and a buzzard's high pitched cry, far above. If we look up into the gaps between the treetops we can see that big brown bird made tiny by distance, circling on a thermal. Then another buzzard joins it, and another, and soon their plaintive cries sound together. But closer than their mournful commentary there's a soothing, uplifting sound filtering through; water! Now the path takes us steadily downwards to a stream running through the wood. We can hear it plashing and gurgling over the stones as we descend and the mineral tang of the brook reached us.

Eagerly we reach its edge and stoop to scoop up that crystal water. As its cool benediction, infused with sparkling sunlight, caresses our tongue we think:

'Bless me holy water. Refresh me and be refreshed, from the Source of All Being.'

We sprinkle droplets onto our eyes and say:

'May no impurity taint this precious flow or contaminate my insight.'

Then we touch our wet fingers to our forehead, and say:

'May truth bubble up in me as from the wellspring of All Knowing'.

We savour the moment, seeing our own otherworldly reflection in the swift moving stream. Perhaps our wild self looks the same as we do in 'ordinary reality', perhaps not.

We know that our special glade is on the other side of this bright water so we now need to look for a place to cross. Turning we follow the brook westward, delighting in its companionable babbling. Silvery fish dart underneath the shimmering mirror of its surface, occasionally surfacing with a plop. The brook widens now and we pass a grey heron wading out to fish. It eyes us warily but, detecting no threat, resumes its stately stepping through the shallows. Then an iridescent kingfisher darts by and draws our attention to three deliberately placed flat stones.

We step out onto the first large stone. With each step we'll be going deeper into this wild reality, moving further from our daily cares. The steps are widely spaced and we almost have to jump.

'One, deep into the green,
Two, deeper into the green,
Three, deeply into the green'

And we're across, moving through a fringe of reeds onto springy turf, disturbing a water vole as we go.

But what's this? Now we're faced with a hawthorn thicket stretching off in both directions. Is there a passage through? It seems not. Nor under or over, unless we want to be torn to shreds. The tender young leaves and pretty blossom may create a pleasing picture but beneath lie dark spikes that would rend us. Does this mean we must turn back?

Perhaps not. For if we ask these formidable trees politely then there may be safe passage granted.

We bow low to the prickly bushes, sensing their astute and inscrutable air.

'May I pass though, marvellous beings?'

We wait. Maybe we need to recognise their magic.

'May I pass though, mysterious beings?'

This time we acknowledge their pert nature.

'May I pass though, mischievous beings?'

A robin alights on a gnarly branch, cocking its head and bobbing. We look at it and when we look back a way has cleared, just a little. If we're careful we can creep along the narrow passage between the spiky boughs. We edge forward, mindful of the prickling that's part playful, part intimidating. Perhaps with regular visits, these trees will feel more amenable to our presence and give us more leeway.

They guard something special so can't be blamed for making us prove our worth.

For now we edge forward cautiously until we're through the tangled tunnel. Before us is another obstacle; a grassy bank strewn with fresh pink and white daisies. Undeterred we climb it and run lightly down the other side, straight through a gap between two ash trees and into a clearing. We spin around, gazing in wonder at the ancient beech and oaks that guard the edges of this glade. Beyond their formidable, but benign, presence the woodland now seems darker, more brooding. In the distance there's a loud crack of a branch as if an unfeasibly large creature has passed through.

This is the primal wildwood; daunting yet fiercely protective of those who respect it.

Here at the centre, surrounded by those defensive green beings, all is safe and calm. There's a circle of lush grass with a huge rock in the middle. We walk to it and rest our hand onto its sun-warmed surface, tracing the swirls of grey-green lichen and the pits worn over time by countless drops of rain. These dips and hollows fit our fingertips exactly. We raise our face to the benediction of the sun in the cloudless blue and feel a surge of nameless joy, as if we've finally come home.

Oh yes, this is the place!

Here's our wildwood sanctuary, our place between worlds. Here we can dance with our untamed self; with our *unseen* companions, our creature-teachers and, if they're willing, our faery counterparts...

Here we dance with All-That-Is.

We spend a time in quiet contemplation now, sitting or lying on this special megalith in the deep green heart of our being. We touch, smell, hear and sense all that's around us. In this blissful peace we can access our deepest *knowing*, hearing the clear voice of truth we all possess. We can see visions; hear messages. We can focus on our wildest dreams, making them manifest in 'ordinary reality'. As wild dreamers this *dreaming-into-being* – creating a better life-dream for ourselves and others – is vital. From this place of deep sanctuary we can utilise our Dreamer/Creator nature to positively enhance the energies of the All through our envisioning. In time we'll have meaningful liaisons here, dreaming together with our *unseen* companions...*for the good of the All*. We'll regain the sense of rightness – of sureness and equanimity – that we've been missing for too long.

Whatever we need, we'll unfailingly find it here. For now we just enjoy the beauty of the moment, however it's revealed to us.

When we've concluded our contemplation, or communing, we give thanks and move back through the gap between the two giant ash trees. We climb the grassy daisy-strewn bank and run down the other side. We ask for safe passage though the hawthorn thicket and find that the way has been left open for us to crawl through. When we reach the other side of this prickly tunnel we find the gap has closed behind us, as if it never was. There's a quivering in those bright leaves as if the bushes were sniggering knowingly to themselves. This time they've sprouted crimson berries instead of blossom, just to make sure we're paying attention.

We thank them.

Now we approach the three stepping stones across the water. We pause to admire their pinkish hue under that sparkling, rippling stream. Then:

'One, moving away,
Two, travelling back,
Three, I am returning'

And we're over on the other side.

Now instead of retracing our steps we continue in a clockwise direction, moving back to our starting place via a fresh route. This outward path winds through an old orchard where silent apple trees stoop, some heavy with small hard fruit and dripping lichen, others bearing balls of mistletoe. We glimpse a bent man with a puckered face the colour of rough cider but he merges into a tree, at one with the craggy bark. We send him our good wishes and move onwards.

Yet again the way ahead is obscured, this time by broad hairy creepers of twining ivy and honeysuckle that trail across the path and drape down. Stepping over the snaking vines and moving them aside methodically, we find that rather than thinning out our way is choked by a tangle of brambles and briars. The wild rose petals may be blush pink and their heady scent beguiling but their dark thorny branches block out the daylight. Is there a way round the challenge? No, our route goes this way; the track disappears into the thicket ahead. We can't barge through as we'd be snagged, tripped up and ensnared. The wildwood's clearly confronting us: *do we really wish to return to superficial modern reality and leave our wildness behind?* It seems we need to clarify our position.

'*I came to the wildwood with respect, now I seek to leave with honour. I've a purpose in the human world but will always return to this place of my heart. Grant me passage through and I'll carry your wild enchantment with me, spreading it wherever I go.*'

We pause, alert to any change. Gradually, there's a shift in the greenery, the branches imperceptibly forming themselves into a tunnel. Giving thanks, we crouch, almost on all fours, and move laboriously through the narrow gap. As we go forward, bowed and cautious, we acknowledge that there's no malice here, only a test of our intentions, but still the ducking down is hard. Just as we fear we can't lean forwards any longer we're out again, blinking in daylight with graceful young trees lining the path instead of twisted undergrowth. There's a chiffchaff calling, a tree creeper darting up a trunk and a flurry as a foraging wren flits away. The long shadows of the trunks stretch across the open grass show us how long we've been gone. Or not, for this is a time-out-of-time. Either way we know that we've nearly come full circle, back to the place of our entry into this fabulous realm.

Now we stop, stoop and pick up whatever is beneath our fingers on the track. Our natural token could be a snail shell, empty and almost transparent, a perfect acorn cup or a shard of flint like a Neolithic arrowhead. This symbol of the wild will travel back into the world with us, resonating in our daily lives. We'll treasure the connection it gives us to this place – and the energies we'll carry with us – and then we move on.

Sure enough we soon see the place where the trees part and the meadow starts. As we approach, we see we've come full circle, our path meeting the initial track we took into the wildwood. We feel its insistent tugging within us – the pull into the green heart of being – but know that way's for another time. For now there's another place for us to be; somewhere that needs the essence we bring with us. So we move from the flickering sylvan light of the woods into the midday sun as wiser, kinder beings.

And we follow the flattened track that leads us through cow parsley and rosebay willow herb to the place where we began our journey. With the wildwood behind us we face towards the south, to the glittering sea on the distant horizon. We imagine we can hear the far-away waves and the cries of gulls. With this beauty in our soul we close our eyes, take three deep, slow breaths and open them again, in 'ordinary reality'. We take time to look at our human hands and feet, breathing the scents and hearing the sounds of this world.

Then we go through our grounding procedure.

I suggest that as part of our grounding we write up our experience in a journal.

Making notes is recommended as it's amazing how much symbolic information, as well as literal guidance, crops up and we may not realise its meaning until later. We may think we'll always remember our fantastic journeys but there's a wealth of fine detail we could overlook in retrospect.

Sustainable Development

So, that was my framework. I hope it proved inspirational for developing a personalised version. I've made a recording of it so you can practice journeying and build confidence for creating your own. It's available via www.poppypalin.org.

As we develop, we'll find that our place – and its inhabitants – take on a life of their own. For example, other birds will start calling. Maybe they'll even land on our outstretched finger. They could be as commonplace as a sparrow, or otherworldly and fantastic. We might hear those badgers stirring and find an inquisitive snout emerging from a den. We may encounter stoats, hedgehogs or foxes – or mythical creatures like a winged horse or golden swan to carry us over that tricksy hawthorn thicket.

There can be seasonal (or unseasonal) fluctuations. Instead of bluebells there may be snowdrops, anemones and celandines or a swirl of spice-coloured autumn leaves hiding fanciful fungus and thick mud. There may be the glitter of frost on hard earth, a dusting of snow on bare branches, or a frozen stream under a full moon. Trees may be budding, dew-clad at dusk or dawn. Both fruits and flowers may be seen on one bush. These changes needn't follow our earthly seasons but can echo a personal phase or feelings. If it pleases us we can have all seasons in one visit! These changes can be directed by us or can surprise us.

This is a living landscape, after all.

Although we began with an authentic native experience, it's fine if our wildwood becomes enchanted with silver fruit that tinkle like bells and exotic magenta blooms that sound like trumpets. It

74

can be *Alice in Wonderland* meets *National Geographic*. Anything goes as long as it feels like a cohesive, convincing reality to us.

And it has to feel authentic, otherwise we won't feel comfortable about the next stage, which is deliberately inviting another being – our wild companion – into our space.

CHAPTER FOUR
Wild Reunion

'Your loneliness is an illusion...and your sadness only the cold fog of your forgetting. *We're a particular point of* remembering *for you; a way for you to experience an endless, marvellous truth. Not alone; ALL ONE.'*

From Inner Guidance

'There's only One Light and 'you' and 'me' are holes in the lampshade.'
Mahmud Shabistari

'Everybody is fundamentally the ultimate reality.'
Alan Watts

Now that we've used our Creator skills to bring a sanctuary to life we can invite our special guests there.

We'll notice that at the beginning of each part of this book – and indeed this chapter – there's a quote from Inner Guidance. Our Wild Dreaming Self is one such inner guide, focussed through our soul.

But what is the soul?

Soul Love

Defining a fluid concept like the soul can only be done by analogy. I have two that work for me:

1. *Infinite Consciousness is the Great Spirit – that is, All Energy.* This Spirit-energy snakes sinuously into each (apparent) physical experience like fingers into a glove. Each individual experience creates an energetic fingerprint, or lingering psychic impression, on the Great Spirit. This unique imprint is the soul. The imprint may seem singular but it is as much a part of the Great Spirit as our own fingerprints are part of our greater body.

2. *The Infinite Ocean of Consciousness is made up of many energetic spirit droplets.* These become coloured, or flavoured, by our particular experiences...thus becoming souls. As much as these souls seem different and distinct, they're still part of the great sea of awareness, hence our innate ability to access eternal wisdom. We're never really separate from our Source because we are as much It as a droplet is the ocean. We hold It's Mystery within us just as it absorbs our unique energies and experiences in the greater ebb and flow of existence.

If we realise our true nature then the inherent understanding of our soul-self is available to us at all times, providing excellent one-to-one guidance. All we need do is become intimate with our inner voice and refer to it as we would our most trusted confidant.

We'll find this so much easier when we've begun entering the silence *regularly.*

As adults we've become habituated to other voices, the haranguing of external and internal criticisms and worries. We search for answers outside of ourselves, giving little credence to our own profound *knowing*. Self-reliance is regarded as conceited and talking to our self considered imbalanced when it's quite the reverse. We become disempowered by heeding prevailing opinions instead of our gentle internal, eternal voice. The more we *enter the silence* the more this voice can be heard, calm and familiar, in the spaces between the chatter in our lives. By deliberately tuning back in to our primary frequency we'll gradually eliminate the static and access our essential signal, broadcasting sweet and true.

Or as true as it can be when operating through an (apparent) physical body in a dense realm.

Like fresh spring water collecting minerals as it filters through rock, our signal can never be pure as it was at Source. Because of this filtering I suggest we need a second opinion or a different – wider, deeper – perspective. I advocate establishing a relationship with another being that's chosen to work with us on our earth-walk. It'd be a waste not to utilise this generously given assistance.

But who might these benevolent beings be?

Who's Who

These beings can be either:

- Discarnate – *not currently embodied, between physical lives*
- Incarnate – *embodied but not in this dense dimension of reality*

If a being is discarnate – free of bodily restrictions – then obviously they're less 'filtered' than we are and their guidance will be purer. If they're incarnate, but at a subtler level of being – operating at a higher frequency – they'll have access to a more refined, enhanced perspective than we currently have.

These guiding beings can be any of the following:

- Human – *a discarnate person that once lived on Earth, as we seem to now*
- Animal – *a discarnate creature that once lived, to whom we feel an affinity*
- Faery – *a discarnate or incarnate Fey being from another Earth race, such as a pixie*
- Elemental – *an earthly energetic representative expressing land, fire, air or water*

- Green Being – *an energetic representative/spirit of particular plants, trees etc.*
- Unearthly – *an incarnate or discarnate 'alien' from another planet/dimension*

We could meet another variety of being not mentioned here as there are no limits. The only certainty is that our inner – or psychic/intuitive – guides work at an energetic, or non-material, level. We could say it's an *immaterial* level but this word now means irrelevant, which sums up attitudes to that which isn't readily observable, or 'provable'. The beings we meet will be immaterial in the true sense: *they don't have a body we can physically discern in our world.*

If our companion is an incarnate being from another realm, we'll perceive them as they appear there. If we've a discarnate guide then essentially they're the wild essence of themselves and can choose how they appear, putting on a guise that'll attract or reassure us. Perhaps this appearance will be one they 'wore' in another existence when we knew them or be taken from a period/culture/mythos we enjoy. We'll more readily recognise, and relate to, a guide that appears familiar/appealing than if they're an amorphous energetic emanation. Once again it isn't the appearances that matter – although they can be enjoyable – but the message they'll convey.

One thing that our companion guides tend not to be is our deceased relatives. Before we continue I'll explain why, in my experience, this isn't the case.

Bring Out Your Dead?

Despite appearances there's no such thing as death, just a shift in our point of perception.

Once our bodily identity is dropped our awareness can leave this realm. If we've *remembered* our true nature, or finished learning in our singular soul-role, then the 'game of life' is up and our wild dreaming self will integrate back into the Oneness of the Wild Dreaming Self. Some call this reaching Nirvana as it's the bliss of absolute (re)union.

Sometimes we *remember* but want to continue our individual learning experience. We'll undergo a 'debriefing' at an *unseen* level with other willing souls, assimilating our knowledge and considering our options. We then choose another life-dream – what we call *reincarnation*.

Yet sometimes a soul is so habituated to its *forgetting* that it unwittingly becomes stuck in the life-dream cycle of (apparent) death and rebirth, refusing to experience anything outside of that paradigm. It reincarnates involuntarily; continuously. Such an unconscious, somnambulist soul can identify so strongly with its physicality that at the point of death it refuses to leave. Its disembodied energy will then 'haunt' the manifest realm it identifies with. This energetic emanation can sometimes be picked up by us just as the radio programme we're tuned to can be broken into by other nearby stations. Mostly it'll be imperceptible, lost between the 'bandwidths' of seen and *unseen* realities...so near and yet so far.

Whatever the soul's scenario, when awareness leaves the body the effect is like a computer shutting down; the information that was displayed through the PC is now unavailable to those left behind. The individual information hasn't ceased to exist but is inaccessible to anyone in the physical world of the defunct body/ computer. Yet for a brief period our 'source code' – our unique etheric resonance – can still transmit itself to the living. It's our last broadcast before our transmission is no longer available at this frequency and it says '*I still exist; I'm okay*'.

Sometimes we may transmit a recognisable scent, at other times a word or sound – perhaps laughter or a familiar cough. We may move an object or send an apport – a meaningful item that seemingly appears from nowhere. If possible we may even transmit an energetic imprint of our previous physical selves – an after-image.

Here are three personal examples of this communication:

1. An old friend died recently and later my car filled up with the smell of a distinctive antiseptic. It wasn't an ordinary scent, generated by explicable means, but rather a *psychic* scent that could be perceived physically. As soon as I understood this was my friend passing on his message the scent completely vanished. I later found out that he'd had that antiseptic applied regularly when in the hospice.

2. Myself and a partner had our guinea pigs die on the same day. As we sat grieving we suddenly had their biscuity smell of warm hay wafted under our noses, as if an invisible hand had held up their bedding to us both simultaneously.

3. A friend had to euthanise her frail elderly cat and was distraught at her decision. That night the (now able bodied) cat jumped onto her bed. And as if to prove it wasn't her imagination the cat came the next night too. Then never again.

I'd imagine most people have communication experiences of this kind, we just don't discuss them. How much quicker we'd all *remember* if we did! Yet if no such message is forthcoming this doesn't mean the 'outgoing' being didn't care. The thrill of being unencumbered by physicality – and released from any pain – means we hasten away, elated at being our true expansive selves again. We forget we've been human as easily as we once forgot our Infinitely Consciousness Self! For us to expect a liberated soul to reappear later and 'perform' is like expecting our PC to keep running a particular programme after we've deleted it. Or like trying to force a genie back into the restrictive bottle when it realises how powerful it is uncontained. At a later stage, an intermediary – an *unseen* companion acting as emissary – may step in to offer comfort. But generally once we've left the particular bodily building we inhabited we've no reason to return.

We know we're all One and we'll be reunited soon enough.

However, as with all things *unseen* there're contradictions. Our relatives *can* continue to make themselves known, sometimes many years after they relinquished their human identity.

Recently a friend told me her father, many years deceased, still makes contact when there's something momentous happening in her life. On hearing he was still 'popping in' her mother commented '*but wouldn't he have reincarnated by now?*' to which my friend gave the sensible reply '*we're multi-dimensional beings and so there's no reason why his essence can't function on several levels at once.*' Linear time doesn't exist except as a human concept to keep order. Our essence exists concurrently before we were 'born', when we 'live' and after we 'die'.

Everything is everything else, happening simultaneously!

Awareness operates in the eternal *Now*, beyond any limited law we impose on it.

Anything's possible! How can it not be when we're All Possibility?

And so it is possible our *unseen* companion will be a relative, but not likely. In my experience our companions are beings who fully *remember* and have consciously opted to do this specialist work. They're not so far removed from our lives as to be aloof but their objective response isn't affected by any lingering familial associations. They're adept at *attached detachment*. As wild spirituality is about challenging assumptions, and is experiential, the only way to understand this better is to make our own enquiries. To do this safely I suggest we follow the guidelines here.

Guiding Light

Often, communication with 'the spirits' means Ouija boards, séances and careless 'channelling' which lead people straight to the low etheric realms. As we've previously noted the entities at those levels can be tricksters or vampires, the energies disturbed and the souls there lost, as in those who 'haunt'. Hence the dearth of wise counsel they can offer. Going to them is like venturing down a dark alley outside a pub and expecting the man urinating against a wall to discuss Wittgenstein. Perhaps he will but more likely there's trouble in it. And why go down there when there's a debating society in a brightly lit hall on the other side of the street?

Here we'll by-pass the lower realms and aim our attentions at the clear energies of those who've chosen to advise and support – our *unseen* wild companions. They dwell close to us but have the expertise to remain apart from the troublesome etheric that immediately surrounds us. They've a direct line to Infinite Consciousness and can access the bigger picture whilst also empathising with our incarnate state. They've studied in astral University – a further education after our earthly life-school experience – and are qualified for the task of mentoring. They work for us but also for their own development...*and the good of the All.*

Companions never interfere but gently support, which is why they're also known as a *guide*. They offer us *guidance* that helps us grow to our fullest potential.

A companion guide is:

- *A caretaker*: one who'll work on our energetic field to heal and protect
- *An escort*: a travel courier that ensures our safe Otherworldly journeys
- *A conduit*: a refined link between the dense human level and the *unseen* beyond
- *A teacher*: one whose wisdom comes from experience and being closer to Source
- *A counsellor*: a dedicated adviser who'll help us work through our problems
- *A key-worker*: one that's got our case notes and is acting as an advocate

All these attributes are strengthened when we both acknowledge and work with them with sensible expectations.

This means we should bear in mind that a genuine *unseen* companion isn't:

- *A dictator*: they'll never demand or seek control
- *A god*: they don't want worship, only respect
- *A saviour*: they can help with, but not prevent, every human learning experience
- *Our slave*: this is an equal relationship, not a master/servant scenario

84

- *A prophet:* probabilities/patterns can be noted but everything's mutable
- *Completely infallible:* they've got the bigger picture, not absolute knowledge or control

Like belly buttons everybody's got a companion. Sometimes we've more than one, perhaps even a small team, and they may change throughout the phases of our life. Their aim is to compliment our prevailing energy, making us comfortable and so more receptive. However, although they're compatible, we get who we are given (although on a deeper energetic level there'll have been an agreement reached between us). Of course, in the greater scheme of things *we're all one* and their separate individuality is illusory. But for the sake of the learning experience we appear to be different and so choice is important.

Because of this we can:

1. *Ask for the companion we're currently allotted to introduce themselves.* Then we can forge a more active relationship with them.
2. *Ask for another companion of the kind we'd like to work with.* As wild spirits, we may want to collaborate with an *unseen* green being such as a member of the Faery races, known collectively as the Fae or Fey. But why?

Faery Stories

The Fey are Earth's unearthliness personified – the most subtle, charming and alarming aspects of the natural world translated into recognisable forms.

It's probable that in our ancient ancestor's time the land was shared with faeries of all kinds. All over the globe, local variations on pixies, sprites, goblins or elves – along with their races or 'courts' – are mentioned in folklore, which is the people's story in allegorical form. These faerytales tell of quirky, enchanting, and utterly capricious beings with a dual nature. They were both ethereal (living in a shining Otherworld parallel to ours) and physical (dwelling on or in the Earth). They were simultaneously eerie (promoting superstitious fear) and earthy (attracting lust and admiration). They could vanish to a place just *beyond* human influence (and take a mortal with them) or live in seclusion in harmonious wild places (interacting only when the whim took them). If so inclined, they could grant wishes.

What was consistent about the Fey was their refusal to be commanded or interfered with. They always dealt harshly with any lack of respect for their boundaries. Yet although they were uncanny, and could be intimidating, their presence made life more magical and they were feted as much as feared.

They're as roguish and beguiling as foxes; dwellers on the boundary of the natural and the unknown...and either loved or loathed for it.

However, over the centuries the manufactured human world became unbearably hostile to their enthralling, and essentially feral, ways. Organised religion and persecution, deforestation, the Industrial Revolution, pollution, devastating wars and the nuclear age saw them pulling away from stifling physicality. They effectively slipped *into* the land itself, to an etheric level *beyond* the invasion of so-called progress yet still close to the physical places they love. This level isn't the low etheric but a much sweeter, faster, more refined realm that shares our space but not our frequency. Let's say our manifest world broadcasts the energetic equivalent of thrash metal and theirs divine symphonies. There may be an interface between our noise and their sublime melodies *but only when they allow it*. They're so much more in tune than the average human that it's easy for them to control reception, tuning us out while living in a parallel wild world.

We can still physically encounter the Fey in the last remnants of uncivilised nature – on the margins – but this is rare, as manifesting in our modern world is like donning a sodden wool overcoat after being accustomed to gossamer. Some Fey are resentful about this, others sad. Yet there're still faery beings that are determined to forge psychic links with wild-spirited humans for the sake of influencing our realm again. If we approach them in the right way – with respect and a little whimsicality – they can be perceived with our inner sight and a relationship forged. Not for kicks as a spiritual tourist but for the sake of meaningful collaboration. They may be fickle to the point of malice but they're also committed if the cause is a good one, such as the preservation of wild ways.

They may also feel inclined to help us if our soul is essentially of a poetic faery nature. As there're no opportunities to physically incarnate into a faery body, we may become a faery soul in a human form. This presents as many difficulties as boons. It is a struggle to be burdened with human limitations, and surrounded by human cruelty, but a blessing to witness reality with deeper poignancy and joy than most people. Alternatively we may have Fey blood, from a time when a human ancestor interbred with a faery being. This genetic inheritance could manifest itself in pointed ears, webbed fingers/toes or long tapering digits. Or it may reveal itself in an uncanny sensitivity or creativity. Either way, having such a link makes it easier for faeries to relate to us. They've a strong sense of kinship and even being partly like them will mean their natural loyalty – and curiosity – will be stirred. The benefits of working with the Fey are huge and surprisingly they work both ways. The main reasons are:

- *To bring renewal.* We both want greening – or re-wilding – of the land. They've got inspiring regenerative ideas; we've the ability to manifestly carry them out
- *To bring healing.* They'll support our work with plants and herbs, helping us 'speak their language'. They want us to live harmoniously, as they do, and will teach us their natural remedies so that their way isn't lost to the world
- *To poeticise our lives.* The Fey are poetry in motion and fabulously inspiring. They love wordplay and will be our muse for their a-*muse*-ment, sharing the en-*chant*-ment of unreasonable rhymes. In Part Three we'll look at the importance of poeticising our lives; now we can ask the Fey to help with it
- *To bring the magic back.* The Fey are both childlike and

87

elegant, their influence being cleansing and uplifting as well as deliciously unconventional. We're a means of reawakening their glamorous, mysterious influence in a prosaic realm and revealing its wonders afresh

Clearly there are great benefits from requesting a Fey companion. The means of meeting them is the same as if we're asking to meet our own allocated guide. We need to follow the procedure for journeying to our wild lair, then adapt it accordingly.

I'll guide you through the process using my version, beginning where we enter the sanctuary in the clearing.

Extending Hospitality

At the centre of this sanctuary, surrounded by those protective, ancient tree-beings, all is calm. We stand in the circle of lush grass with the ancient rock in the middle. We rest our hand onto its sun-warmed surface, tracing the swirls of grey-green lichen and the pits worn over time by countless drops of rain. The dips and hollows fit our fingertips exactly.

This is our place. Here we're safe to call on those who'll help us.

We now visualise our self standing within a circle of protective blue flame. As we look we see its brilliant fire spring up from the earth as if somebody has turned up a gas jet. Each blue tongue is tipped by radiant white-gold and flickers with irrepressible life. Then we imagine another circle of flame appear before us, big enough for another being to stand. We look at this ring of kind-light and know it's secure enough for us to invite our *unseen* companion – either the one we already know, or the one we seek – into.

We now ask with conviction

'I ask that my true companion guide, representative of my highest possible good, please be revealed'

We wait. When an *unseen* being emerges in the circle we shouldn't get too involved in their appearance as these can be deceptive. Sometimes even a genuine companion may appear to shift through several guises, resolving into clarity. Instead of being distracted by the details of their manifestation we point to them, directing our will, and reiterate

'With respect I ask, show yourself truly'

Any genuine *unseen* companion won't find this offensive but will welcome our prudence. It's unlikely that anyone but our true companion will appear as the circle of fire is a protected environment. This is an energetic reality and what we set up energetically, with certainty, is valid and exists. Yet 'belt and braces' is a good habit to get into. *Unseen* beings are much better at disguise than physical ones. In time we'll know immediately if they feel wrong, even if they look right, but for now testing is our only means. So we question again, with compassionate authority, for the third and final time

'With love I ask, show yourself truly'

If the *unseen* being is an imposter then they'll vanish and we can repeat the procedure until our true companion arrives. If no *unseen* being appears for us by the third attempt it's best to leave the exercise for that session and return afresh. This doesn't mean that we've no companion, but rather that prevailing energetic conditions aren't right to make the link. Or that we lack conviction, or feel trepidation. As this is our inaugural attempt there's no precedent established so it may be harder than on subsequent occasions.

Please be assured that we all have an unseen *companion and that they will come!*

However our companion appears to us, their appearance isn't who they are, any more than our clothes are what we are. Generally they'll have done their best to put us at ease with an appearance that interests or delights us. If we're just beginning, they're more likely to choose from a range of personas that are perceived as sagacious, such as Buddhist monk, Native American medicine man, Indian guru or Merlin-esque wizard. Hence the predomination of these beings reported as *unseen* guides! This doesn't mean that our companion is male – spirit is sexless energy that can be translated into any form – but rather that our cultures have favoured men as wise figures. If we're already familiar with each other, our *unseen* companion may decide to challenge us a little, moving us away from our comfort zone. But they won't go out of their way to repel or intimidate, as this will be counterproductive. It's always what they communicate that matters, not their costume or looks.

When we've made contact with our companion guide, and they're standing in the circle of flame, what do we say to them?

Small Talk Gets Bigger

Unless we hit it off immediately, the first few meetings are for basic acquaintance, not for discussions on the nature of reality. That comes later!

For now let's think of this like meeting somebody we've been talking to 'online'. This is apt as unbeknownst to our day-to-day self we've probably been having an *etheric* relationship with our *unseen* companion before meeting them. We may've been quite intimate in cyberspace/the ether but now we're face-to-face we'll want to get the measure of each other again. Indulging in small talk – names, where we come from, what we consider our role to be etc. – gives us chance to take stock. How does our companion sound or move? Do they have a scent? What's their predominant energy; for example, is it ebullient, languid or pensive?

This isn't a balanced relationship as it would be with a manifest friend. The *unseen* timescale/frame of reference isn't comparable to ours and doesn't generate trivial gossip. A companion's in the teacher/counsellor role and so will listen more, not expecting us to reciprocate. They're centred on our education as we're the ones engaged in life-school and the challenges of (apparent) physicality. However, asking for them for any news/views shows consideration. Guides are volunteers, not martyrs, and if all we do is demand and devalue them they may be disinclined to continue. Our appreciation for their generosity, and our full attention to their teaching, shows our time together is precious.

As we become more tuned in to each other, and relaxed into

the process, we can broaden our conversational repertoire. Our companions are always most erudite when discussing universal/ personal energies, offering incisive guidance about the meaning of life, and our lives in particular. They aren't at their best when asked for specific predictions or information about world affairs. Probabilities and possibilities are fine to discuss – *what if's* are ideal – but not absolutes such as *when, where and who*. They deal in broad brushstrokes, not meticulous detail.

This isn't because they're phoney or incompetent but because they're without a manifest body and so experience a fascinating multi-faceted reality. Temporal things don't hold them in thrall as they do us. Although they empathise with our concerns, it's the *energies* behind problems that interest them; the patterns, not the minutiae. They witness existence as an etheric flow, not a fixed line, and in a fluid *Now* all futures are subject to change. But although they're more aware, they still haven't returned fully to the Source and so still have an individual – and so limited – perspective, even if it's broader than ours. If we're currently at the rim of the Wheel of Life then our companions are a spoke connected to the hub. It's only at the hub – the Source – that we experience everything concurrently and know all there is to know without the limitations of a particular perception.

There's another reason why asking our companions for specific information isn't advisable and that's because of *our* fallibility. When we want to hear something – the name of the next President, when we'll meet our true love, if our son will pass his final exams – we've stopped being open and the transmission distorts through the filter of need. We'll hear whatever we expect, not what's being said. Yet when we ask about eternal truths and potentiality we're receptive, not anticipating a particular answer.

That's why our companions are guides, not dictators of absolutes or oracles.

If our relationship is built on lively discussion then our lives will be enriched and we won't be disappointed. Our companions will gain by knowing eternal wisdom is being disseminated into this world, through us. It's a win-win situation.

We can meet in our wild sanctuary as suits both parties. As we feel more confident we'll be able to meet without the circle of blue flame simply by asking our companion to reveal themselves truly to us. Then we're more at liberty to wander where we will and perhaps enjoy new experiences outside our created realm, going on educational/inspirational journeys. When we've finished a session we can part company by saying something like:

'May you keep what's yours and may I keep what's mine, returning to our own realms but never really parted. May our link remain until we renew it here again. Go well!'

This gives the companion leave to exit the circle in their own way. Then we can follow our route back to 'ordinary reality' from the lair. In my version this is through the wildwood. Once back we ground ourselves by writing up our experiences and any guidance received.

These one-to-ones in the sanctuary are important. They develop our imagination through visualisation and strengthen our ability to focus, providing a bright thread of continuity in our lives. Yet we may also wish to commune with the companions in more in depth. This we can do through written guidance or *dialogue*.

Words of Wisdom

Dialoguing compliments our journeying. It allows us to have more involved conversations and provides a useful record of our progress. It's how I gained the insights that're interspersed throughout this book as *inner guidance*.

Dialogue allows us to go into fascinating subjects in more depth, including:

- *The nature of reality*: our perception of time/space; matter and (apparent) physicality; dimensions and *unseen* realms; synchronicities
- *The nature of energy*: how the life-force functions/reveals itself; how we may best work with the creative impetus behind Creation

- *The nature of the Self:* the Wild Dreamer and the wild dreamer; holding dual awareness of our collective One and individual one aspects
- *The nature of life and death:* how a soul comes into being; the meaning/purpose of incarnation; where we may go between lives; the soul's imprinted patterns; returning to Source
- *The nature of good and evil:* understanding and valuing the positive/negative aspects of Creation; fear and love; learning acceptance and how not to be; the importance of balance

As we can see, dialoguing is for the big issues we thought we'd never grasp in this lifetime. It's also for advice pertaining to our personal development.

Even though we may not have a specific question in mind we'll need a subject area before we begin, otherwise we'll find that our eager companions will ramble 'off topic'. Our *unseen* friends haven't our time restraints or physical limitations and can offer continual philosophical discourse if we allow it. Having no focus would be like putting a word into an Internet search engine, then wading through the thousands of results. There'd be something pertinent in there for us but have we got the energy or inclination to find out where?

To engage with our companion all we need is a theme for discussion, a reliable pen and a pad of A4 blank paper. We'll use these to ask our questions and take down 'cosmic dictation'.

First we go through our protective procedure. Then we *enter the silence* and relax ourselves by centring on our breath. Then we focus or inner attention on our companion and either invite them into our circle of flame or mentally ask them to come into our sphere of influence, saying something like:

'Dear companion (give name if known) that comes for my highest good, draw close to me now for the purpose of discussing (name the subject/ask the question). I ask this that I may learn and grow, becoming a more effective part of the All. If it's your will, as it is mine, so may it be.'

Or we can open our eyes and write this invitation at the top of our page. Then we wait to feel the presence of our companion, allowing the pen's tip to rest lightly on the paper.

The communication may happen in three ways:

1. *The dictation method:* we'll hear our companion's familiar voice speak to us in our mind. If so we can write down what we hear.

2. *The automatic method:* we'll feel the need to write without consciously knowing what will be said, the pen having a 'life of its own'.

3. *The inspired method:* we'll see imagery/symbolism/words and write down what we're shown.

No one way is better, indeed we may find there's a mixture of approaches. Again it's the *substance* that's important.

We shouldn't worry if this process is influent at first. Conversely we may find we're left with a sore hand as reams of information pours forth. Even though our companion has the most say, this is a conversation, not a lecture, and so we need to punctuate their flow with responses or requests for clarification. To help this we can swap pens for questions and answers, perhaps between green and black ink, which also helps discern who said what afterwards. We need to get into a rhythm that suits both communicator and receiver and the only way to do this is by practice, creating a format that suits both parties.

If we find we can't get results using this active method, we can try the inactive method; that is, using our non-dominant hand to write our answers. If we're right-handed then we write our questions with that hand and then swap hands to get answers with our left hand. This allows our conscious self to step back and for the process to be controlled by instinct, not intellect. Results can be messy to begin with but in time there's little difference between hands.

Soon we'll come to recognise our companion's idiosyncratic ways of speech. They can often sound quaint or foreign, perhaps because of the imprint of an important incarnation. Or they may think we'll take them more seriously if they sound archaic, age equating to wisdom. They're also as prone to repeating certain phrases as we are, such as *'again I say...'* or *'therefore it's like this...'* Rather than finding these quirks irritating we can think of them as calling cards that verify authenticity.

Just as trance isn't a defenceless daze, dialoguing isn't possession. It's a careful, directed exchange between two consenting beings, not the indiscriminate 'downloading' of information from unknown, unauthorised sources. Such ill-advised 'fishing' for wisdom means we're placing trust in the infallibility and integrity of all *unseen* beings, just because they're *unseen*.

Being disembodied, or non-human, doesn't necessarily make us wise or kind.

If we can't expect significant insights from a random passer-by in the physical world then we can't expect it in the non-physical realms. One aspect reflects the other, always. I say this as once we've learned how effective this method is, we may be tempted to contact other disembodied sources. Imploring other voices to come through can be compulsive, primarily because there're other unscrupulous forces doing the compelling. Like an alcoholic believing the results of drinking this next bottle will be better we may think that if we keep trying we'll make an amazing link sooner or later.

More likely we'll hook an old boot masquerading as the mythic salmon of wisdom...and it may not let us throw it back easily.

I only ever advocate contacting our approved, tried-and-tested companions. They can tell us all we need to know and if they don't know something themselves they'll find out on our behalf. They can even bring another trusted being in with them. We never need leave their security for the sake of something more sensational. That'd be like switching our computer's firewall off to look at restricted sites for a thrill.

If we wouldn't do that why do the energetic equivalent?

Chatter Matters

Receiving dialogue is stimulating and visiting our wild sanctuary is nourishing. Yet once we're acquainted with our companion we don't need a formal arrangement to keep in touch. When we recognise their energetic imprint, or frequency, we can 'tune in' to them any time for a chat.

All we need do is visualise our regular protective bubble and then in our mind's eye provide a circle of blue flame for our companions to step into. Once we're familiar with this process it should take no more than minutes to complete. Then we can mentally ask for our familiar *unseen* friend to commune with us 'on the go'. We can have an internal conversation anywhere in this fashion.

This isn't like talking to our eternal self but rather like a conversation with any close human friend, the sort who doesn't have to even tell us their name when we answer the phone. We can recognise their tone immediately and ease into a familiar mode with them. As with a trusted human confidant we can talk about anything and everything without pressure. It's like a catch-up before we meet properly, enabling us to chew over what's immediately happening to us, such as an observation on a bus journey, a realisation as we walk down the road or an incident at work. Having the reassurance of such camaraderie with us wherever we go – be that high moor, post office queue or prison cell – is invaluable. I hope this section has offered enough reasons for us to strengthen our links with the *unseen* beings that walk alongside us. Because although we all have our own innate wisdom, life's more meaningful and fulfilling when we share it with a trusted friend.

'Do you remember the solitary man in Beijing, deliberately standing
in front of the oncoming tanks to stop them?
Isn't it wonderful that we're all that brave man, whether we know it
yet or not?
He is who we are. Yet our individual expressions of courage,
determination and love will be revealed in infinite other ways.
Perfect!'

From Inner Guidance

PART TWO
Dedication

'They sing that every single point of view,
Each little 'I' that gazes so astounded,
Is consciousness condensed as me and you,
The 'I' of all, eternal and unbounded.'

Author unknown

'...Dismiss whatever insults your soul and your flesh
Shall be a great poem and have the richest fluency
And not only in its words but in the silent lines of its lips...'

Walt Whitman

'My free soul may use her wing.'

George Herbert

CHAPTER FIVE
Expanding Our Embrace

'Once we realise that the nature of our existence is beyond thoughts and emotions, that it is incredibly vast and interconnected with all otherbeings, then the sense of isolation, separation, fear and hopes all fall away. It's an incredible relief!'

Jetsumno Tenzin Palmo

'Don't say 'this inanimate being has no awareness'.
It does – it is you who have no awareness!'

Ahmad Lbn Ata Allah

'Never, never be afraid to do what's right; especially if the well-being of a person or animal is at stake. Society's punishments are small compared to the wounds we inflict on our soul when we look the other way.'

Martin Luther King

'Strive to survive causing the least suffering possible'.

Flux of Pink Indians

Now we've companionship on our journey we can focus on living in awareness, with integrity and authenticity. This is the wild-spirited way – the pathless path that leads us deeper into the green heart of being. Before we set off again let's consider that verdant centre again.

Crux of the Matter

Because we're concerned with wildness, be that of the spirit – the wild essence – or of the wider world, our focus is resolutely green...the colour of burgeoning, untamed life on Earth. Preserving and encouraging this wild life in any way we can is vital to us. And because we're concerned with becoming the most empathetic, responsive being we can be we move to the rhythm of our heartbeat drum – the tender throb at the core of a compassionate life.

Part Two is all about centring ourselves in this green-hearted life. It advocates a combination of our inner journeying and our generous, wise actions in 'ordinary reality', encouraging us to hold the balance between our individual, temporary one and collective, eternal One aspects. The concepts contained in this segment are challenging but if we persevere, it they'll connect us more fully to each other, to all other beings and to the land...and so ultimately to Infinite Consciousness.

They'll bring us back to our Self.

Well look at three essential aspects, or ways of being, that'll help with this Great Reunion. These are:

- *Honouring*: living our truth in accordance with our *remembering*
- *Observing*: being a conscious and sensitive witness
- *Loving*: practicing unconditional acceptance and living carefully

Let's begin the next part of our journey by focussing on *honouring*.

102

Yes, Your Honour

When considering this first aspect I contemplated my own honour, both what it means and how it's expressed. I did this contemplating, as I so often do, when out in the living landscape. My walking becomes a mobile meditation and I breathe deeply, in measured awareness of each step. Even as I relax into this natural cadence I become hyper-vigilant of the scents/sounds/sensations of nature. When I'm in a calm and receptive state, in sync with my own pulse and that of my environs, my inner guidance flows beautifully and I often find – or rather, provide myself with – symbolic answers as I go.

On this occasion I was approaching an ancient embankment which was lined with hawthorn trees, as many untamed places are. As I approached the first tree in the row I instinctively offered it three of the snack raisins in my pocket. It seemed like a spontaneous honouring to me. But was it? Was I doing it un-self-consciously, without expectations, or offering the raisins as a superstitious placatory gesture that could bring me luck or protection? I considered this as honestly as I could as it seemed important. No, I wasn't trying to curry favour or ward off ill-wishing. In fact I didn't want anything at all. Instead I believe my motivation was twofold:

1. *I wanted to represent a human-kind that knows the intrinsic value of its vital green counterparts, with trees as our equal participants in the life-dream.*
2. *I wanted to give a present, as friends do. Yes, I could've transmitted unconditional love through my energetic presence, without having to do anything – in fact I hope my very being expresses a loving intent. But I also enjoy showing my affection.*

As with the honouring at Glastonbury Tor described in my Introduction, this gifting was pure without being pious... respectful and playful both. Those raisins were all I had and so I gave them with appreciation, impulsively.

Granted the tree had no choice in the giving but it wasn't an offensive gift, rather an organic bio-degradable one. If the tree chose to reject the energy of my giving – for the energy is what was being offered for them to absorb – then at least a passing bird or insect may benefit. There was no harm done and perhaps another shining etheric bridge built between me and those perceived as *other*...my other selves.

Just as I recognise my fellow humans I aim to acknowledge the green beings I encounter when out walking. It doesn't matter if a passing jogger looks askance at me talking to the twisted hawthorn I've known for years. Or a dog walker wonders why I'm sharing my bottle of water and cereal bar with a familiar gorse bush. My courtesy isn't *human-centric*. Human-centricity divides us from our wild kin, just as ego-centricity divides us from our human kin. Nor is my courtesy based in temporal considerations like conventional behaviour. It's showing what my priorities are and what I hold dear, beyond any mundane mores.

So, giving honour isn't about pacifying or praising for an ulterior motive. Or about elevating others for what they do. It's about respecting who we truly are, whilst *acknowledging all others as who we are too*...even as we enjoy their (apparent) individual aspect. When we honour we're communicating *I care for you, whoever you appear to be*. It's a statement of willing interdependence: *as you are, so I am*. The aim is to turn our lives into a continual honouring; a fluid gifting of our esteem for our counterparts in the life-dream. But how do we do this, in actuality? Clearly we can do it through considered, considerate deeds but another way is through the generous, melodious language we use.

I'm focusing on this aspect here as it's greatly overlooked.

Poeticise Your Life

Performing all tasks, no matter how insignificant they may seem, with heart – a heart capable of cradling all creation tenderly within it – is essential to the wild spirit. But although the deeds are as vital as life-blood so are the words that describe them.

As you may've already gathered, I love words. My publisher has likened me to a Victorian antiquarian in my desire to embellish any sentence, which I took as a compliment! I do adore language but it's beyond any desire to be grandiose, rather *because it can make the ordinary fabulous.* Used consciously, with care, it encourages the spirit to a flight of fancy instead of reducing life to a dull ellipsis.

For example, experience how the following adjectives evoke something vivid:

Diaphanous, succulent, ominous, glimmering, brittle, tremulous, parched, opulent.

Now experience how these verbs can embellish everyday life while tantalising the tongue:

Undulate, scuttle, nestle, skulk, embezzle, quash, wriggle, splatter.

I employed many evocative terms in my description of the wild sanctuary. I used a painterly approach with a brimming, fresh palette, quite the opposite of the quick sketch we often settle for. Rather than opting for the instant vocabulary of convenience – making our language lean and mean, or fast and furious – I delved deep for suggestive words that satisfied and stimulated. To me this is a vital part of *honouring* – savouring the beauty of what we're experiencing as we let the right phrase slip to the tip of the tongue; rolling language around the tongue like a bon-bon so we may luxuriate in its sweetness.

This shows respect to our subject as we have to engage fully with the sensation/encounter if we want to describe it well. What we express becomes juicy, piquant poetry inspired by our immediate relationship to the moment, not a snappy summary or hollow reaction.

Soundbites Aren't Nutritious

We all hasten to fill spaces. Sometimes we do it because we think everyone's in a hurry; other times from habit. We reply to each other without due reflection; without hearing what's really being said, or observing what's being expressed. This superficial relating leads to assumptions – and therefore misinterpretations – based on what we think we already know. Other times we snap back with a clever rejoinder, wanting to prove we're quick witted. Waiting until we've something kind or insightful to offer may be preferable but a pithy diatribe typically wins out over judicious observation. Such competitive conversing comes from our reactive ego rather than our responsive core self. Either way the language we use can be glib or trite. It's merely filled a gap; giving the appearance of communication without actual communion.

It dishonours us and those we speak with.

When we're alone we can easily begin mentally griping about what's wrong with us/them/it/everything. If we're not having a debate in our heads we're allowing our precious personal space to be invaded by advertising jingles, popular songs we dislike, the dismal litany of mainstream news and the petty bickering of characters – fictional or 'real' – on television. Their language may be brusque or crude, the tone strident or antagonistic...or perhaps the words are indistinguishable, just a burble. Again this artificial barrage of sound – I call it burbulence – dishonours us, as we become passive absorbers of twaddle. But it also dishonours nature, whose ambient music is overwhelmed. It gives value to what we don't actually respect, above the tranquillity of the unfolding moment.

Seeking profundity beyond the perfunctory and deliberating are essential qualities for a wild-spirited soul-poet. Deliberation means we're *deliberate*; living lucidly, on purpose. A wild spirit enjoys a leisurely pace of life, valuing hand-crafting, slow cooking, reflection, solicitude and stillness. Not due to fearful Luddite tendencies, or indolence, but because of *care*. Care as in attention and loving consideration, not worry. Being *care-full* is key to all we do as it centres us in the eternal *Now*, not in some projected future. Rashness, disregard, distraction and the ubiquitous '*whatever*' attitude are the antithesis of this. Those qualities reflect a shallow life of instant gratification just as popping a pill (rather than dealing with the root cause) or eating 'fast food' does.

Language is in danger of becoming uniformly 'fast' also. With email and instant or text messaging, communication is reduced to a bare scrape of meaning across the bread of life. This abbreviated form is like continually boiling down a soup until it's reduced to an unpalatable residue. I'm not advocating a shunning of liberating social media, but rather an *awareness* of what we're doing and a willingness to keep truncated techno-talk in its appropriate place. Otherwise it could easily become the norm and we'll lose the rich heritage of evocative expression that can render the commonplace into something glorious and compelling...a feast, not a famine.

Poeticising is a gentle antidote to the more anodyne aspects of modernity and an acknowledgment of our role as co-creators of a beautiful reality. Using descriptive words in our interactions is a way of expressing our love of life and the thrill of being a unique creative being.

It gives honour.

Mind Your Language

Words can bring lustre to the everyday, allowing the most meagre, familiar interaction to glint and glisten.

In fact, they're magical.

By magical I mean positively and surprisingly transformative; life-enhancing and delightful. We'll consider our own wild magic in Chapter Eight. For now let's consider the enchantment of words and how they can both charm and cause harm, whether intentionally or not.

Communicating in a responsive, conscious way begins with an identification of language that no longer serves our rewilded self, or the world it yearns to co-create. Without knowing it the well-worn phrases that trip from our tongue lock us into a damaged, imbalanced reality we no longer wish to give our energy – or pay lip-service – to. If we're to 'talk our walk' – articulating wild-spirited values in the world – we need to do a bit of self-surgery on our routine speech and dismiss the notion that 'they're only words'.

Because words are powerful and can effectively keep us in separation.

Even the most aware of us use certain dismissive, even derogatory, terms as matter of course – ostensibly because we believe 'actions speak louder than words' and if we don't act on them then they're meaningless. In other eras, words such as 'wog' or 'spastic' would be seen as harmless, but would we find them less offensive if the person only spoke them, without acting out the ignorant bigotry they express? Such divisive words have an effect in the world, their insidious message insinuating rather than bludgeoning. They *resonate*, just as deeds do, only less obviously. Every word has a concept, thought or *energy* behind it. If we give credit to an *unseen* reality then we need to acknowledge the impact of what we put out, be that physically or verbally.

Words can liberate or denigrate, setting the moral tone for a society. Language is an energetic projection representing our personal philosophy or collective outlook.

Care-less talk desensitises and disconnects the user: it diminishes others and consequently ourselves. I'm not suggesting that we humourlessly use 'politically correct' terms and tie ourselves in neurotic knots, rather that we say what we feel as wild spirits and let words mean as much as deeds. By tenderly speaking our inner truth we'll refrain from trivialising, lovingly taking care of the details as to make a better overall picture.

What follows are some everyday – but perhaps unexpected – examples of separatist, and often species-ist – or *human-centric* – language that deserves our consideration. Maybe there aren't any perfect expressions, only more respectful and inclusive ways of expressing familiar concepts. That's our challenge. Let's see what we come up with.

1. **Livestock**. This term states that cows, sheep, pigs etc. aren't creatures in their own right but property – stock – that happens to breathe.

2. **Timber**. Here the dead – and probably deliberately killed – body of a tree is described as nothing but a convenient 'product' for humanity.

3. **Cull**. Would we say *several people were culled by a lone gunman*? Do we have 'serial cullers'? When person has their life taken we call it murder. Why is it any different for any other species?

4. **Roadkill**. We wouldn't leave a human body to be continually run over as if it were litter. Nor would we call them roadkill. We should name the dead creature and if possible move their body to where it can decompose with dignity.

5. **The Environment**. This term suggests a location rather than a living organism, complete with its own non-human denizens and wild ways. Environmentalism denotes concern over something we consider 'out there' and incidental to, not integral to, our existence.

6. **The Natural World**. The inference here is that we're apart from the untamed realm, as if nature is something we visit when it suits us. Do we exist in a separate place...the unnatural world, perhaps?

7. **Scenery**: This word states unequivocally that nature provides a decorative backdrop for human activity.

8. **Renewable Resource**: Materials derived from other living organisms aren't *resources* but stolen personal property. We're all equal expressions of Infinite Consciousness to be worked *with* sensitively, and out of necessity, not materialism.

9. **Put Down/Destroyed**. Euthanasia means a person opting for assisted suicide on health grounds. If a sick or elderly

animal's life is ended then it's also euthanised, not subject to a euphemism or careless brutalism.

10. **Terrorist/Insurgent/Militant**. These divisive words dehumanise people as surely as the term livestock removes the dignified autonomy of animals. '*Six militants were killed*' elicits less sympathy than 'six men'. Insurgents are immediately 'the enemy' – implying we're the force for good. This unhelpful, unhealthy terminology has seeped into our daily lives and become customary.

11. **Those people**. '*Those people always do that sort of thing*'. Yet they *are* us. We're always 'those people' in potentiality!

12. **A Monster**. Certainly we can call abhorrent behaviour – cruelty, torture, degradation – monstrous but that doesn't make the culprit a monster. Again it dehumanises and sets them apart from us. But they're not *other*, just another self acting on something we've decided against.

13. **Behaving like an animal**. Here we're deeming someone's actions less than ours but also demoting animals and making them nefarious...base, bestial and boorish. Or *inhuman,* as if humanity could be held up as the benchmark of compassion. This is lazy language that perpetuates an outmoded hierarchical paradigm.

14. **Pet**. This term reduces a sentient being to less than its 'owner'. 'Companion animal' is a better term yet we need to reconsider the whole concept of captive creatures. There's no place for creatures in cages or tanks unless they're saved from neglect or abandonment by those who've already bought them. If we won't countenance the imprisonment of innocent humans, or their enforced removal from their natural home, why do it to our creature-kin?

15. **Treated like a Guinea Pig**. We've no idea how it feels to be experimented on – often to the death – by a being many times our size that doesn't speak our language and has no respect for us. Every time we trot out the '*...like a guinea pig*'

line we render it anodyne and make the crime acceptable.
This leads me onto the other innocuous seeming terms that mask our human-centric denigration of animals, reinforcing our position as the (apparently) benign rulers of the world.

Animal Writes

Firstly, *leather*. What an innocuous, everyday word it seems.
Yet it conceals a world of cruelty. Leather is another being's tanned skin.
A leather sofa is a skin sofa; that 'butter soft' pair of calf leather boots came at a price higher than the tag. We seem to conveniently disengage from this reality and perceive the cow and the desirable item as separate. We weren't party to the process so deny a connection. That's if we think of the matter at all.

We'd never refer to human skin as leather, suede or a hide. We'd not say that someone's skin was a by product of 'the funeral industry' as we claim leather is of the 'meat industry'. Think of the horror people felt when confronted by the possibility that the Nazis made lampshades from the skins of Jews. Some may find this parallel distasteful but I find it necessary.

We must have universal, not selective, respect and always give the most vulnerable our protection. Because they are us; we are them.
If we find the parallel between the abuse of people and that of animals gratuitously offensive then I suggest we spend time communing with our companions on this subject. If they're truly wild spirits, attuned to the Oneness of Creation, then they'll not support a human-centric view, with delineations as to who/what it's justifiable to mistreat. Evil – or more accurately, *forgetful* behaviour – always stems from our indifference in what we consider to be smaller matters. If we abuse those we deem as 'lesser' then our finer feelings are lost and we're contaminated by our wilful ignorance. Such disregard can't be contained; it seeps, knowing no boundaries. It's only when we have no 'lesser' – or indeed no 'other' – that abuse is indefensible to us. All matters are of similar pressing importance. We'll come back to this subject

111

again in this part of the book. For now it's enough to say that we must face the truth – and the consequences of our choices – without such justifications.

If we decide to wear the skins of our fellow beings then we should name them appropriately and acknowledge our role. A skin doesn't belong to us, or to the slaughterer, but only to the victim. We're thieves and complicit in murder. This doesn't give honour but at least it's honest.

Secondly, there are the words for meat – *pork, bacon, ham, steak,* etc. One step further removed we have *sausages, burgers, joints, chops, mince* which describe without any association to a particular animal. These neat words distance us from the brutal truth of abattoir in the same way as plastic wrapping and polystyrene trays do. The language is as processed as the packaged product it conveniently describes.

When does this desensitising process of denial start? We come into this world with awareness of our Oneness but separation is swiftly established. When young children express curiosity or empathy for other creatures they're shown, and sometimes told, that 'dominion' is their birth-rite. The murder of another being on their behalf is justified as the natural way of things – *the child needs to grow big and strong and they matter most.* They're reassured there's no pain involved *because others don't feel like they do.* It's easy to acquiesce and *forget* when they never actually see the act of murder and the carcass always appears in disguise. When they're inured to the bloody truth can they be blamed for perpetuating the convenient lie themselves?

Yet this collusion, wilful omission and expedient deception has to stop somewhere.

How many children understand where their meat and dairy products, or their clothing come from, let alone the process involved? How many adults have actually grasped the sordid reality and faced up to it? Perhaps if we were routinely exposed to the unpalatable actuality then we could make a more informed, honourable choice. When we seek to live lucidly we can't wilfully

112

remain in an ignorant state, having a selective *remembering*. We need to do our own research, our own facing up.

Because it's disingenuous to want consciousness in some areas of our lives and not others.

We know we're waking up when we realise it isn't possible for something that causes any hurt to be good for us.

Because what harms one harms all.

Supporting a barbaric system – a murder industry – is still supporting it, even at a distance of several times removed. Rearing, killing and preparing animals ourselves may be one thing but allowing someone else to do our dirty work is indefensible, especially when so many meat, dairy and animal skin alternatives are readily available. We're fabulously inventive individuals and have developed an array of cruelty-free replacements, including Lorica for footwear etc. We needn't go barefoot when we ditch meat/dairy, nor become sickly and wan. In fact, every vegan I know is either an athlete or active and robust. This is because most vegan foods are low in fat/high in fibre and also because meals are prepared from scratch, with more care. If proof is needed of the benefits there's plenty of evidence available. The Academy of Nutrition and Dietetics – the world's largest organisation of food and nutrition professionals – concluded that plant-based diets are '*healthful, nutritionally adequate and provide many health benefits in the prevention and treatment of certain diseases.*'

As well as being for our creature-kin, and for us, it's also possible to feed many more people on a vegan diet. Meat and dairy are responsible for high levels of greenhouse gas, pollution and deforestation. I continue justifying but maintain there's no place for polite deliberation when lives are at stake.

Debate is a luxury another creature (another self) can ill afford.

Would we stand back and ponder if an armed gang was going to kill a defenceless man, even if we didn't like the man personally? Or would we take action – any action we were capable of at that moment? Surely what applies to one vulnerable sentient being applies to all? If so we need to act on our compassionate convictions decisively, with alacrity. If we don't feel we can commit fully then we can at least acknowledge our choice and do *something*, working towards relinquishment rather than absolving all responsibility. Because going back to sleep isn't an option for us now; only becoming more deeply awake.

Being vegan is a spiritual choice and an interesting challenge, not a chore. It can do no harm and sets the tone of a life lived honourably. Surely it's worth a try? There's no discredit in trying, only in deliberate avoidance when we know better.

Bringing our physical being into balance with the ethics of our eternal self means our essential energy is no longer blocked or diverted. It makes us more effective, fluent and congruent. Because we've a core understanding of every life-form being equal and interconnected we're more likely to maintain this syncing of spirit and body with a glad heart, not just a sense of obligation. It's about justice for All – for Us; not just us. In such harmony we wield the power of words accordingly; reinforcing our respect by speaking only the kind spell of our truth.

Then we become love-poetry in motion.

We live prayerfully - for allour relations.

Like a Prayer...Only Better

When lived well, with care, our whole life is a paean of praise. Yet with a love of language and an understanding of its potency we can also offer wild words of prayer.

Wild prayers have little to do with what we may've encountered at school or in organised religious ceremonies – or even in our own heads when something goes wrong.

They're not wheedling, placatory petitions or a demonstration of obsequiousness. Nor are they 'canned prayers': formulaic, prescribed and emotionally barren. Instead they're one-off free-form invocations – pure, spontaneous outpourings to the moment.

114

They're heartbeat-poetry.

As soul-poets we can concentrate on life-affirming, luscious words that thrill and evoke. Not for us the bald language of division, nor the insipid banalities of disengagement, but the glorious vocabulary of unity and parity.

Surge, swoop, whorl, lustre, quiver, billow, drench...wild words that well up to the brim of life and spill over. Flourish, cherish, luscious, precious, embrace, beloved...effusive words, as unashamedly tactile as our gestures. Each savoured syllable suggests a phrase to celebrate and liberate.

When we utilise this rich language to pray we're not beseeching a stronger force but communicating with our Infinitely Conscious Self – or to a particular aspect or our Self such as the Fey or creature-kin. Wild prayers are heart-crafted hymns to Creation that elevate any everyday experience to something worthy of tribute. Certainly these inspired statements of intent may focus on a particular outcome in our lives, and so in the wider world, but from a place of empowerment, and deep connection, not helplessness. They both acknowledge, and re-align us with, nature's cadences...*for the good of the All.*

Such a poetic prayer could be:

'By the greening of the ash in May
From sticky black buds bright leaves unfurling,
By the sap drawn up from root to stem
With blushing petals fast uncurling,
As the sun draws up the ripening wheat
That swallows skim on their returning,
So Creation's power is rising,
So my own wildfire is burning,
Warming the seeds of all my dreams,
Bringing to life my deepest yearning.'

Such a prayer is an expression of our delight at spring's burgeoning energy and a longing for our own creativity to bubble up and spill over fruitfully into the world. We're not asking 'the powers that be' to fix it for us, but rather exercising our innate ability as co-creators of a responsive reality. When we focus intentionally and eloquently, we link with All Possibility and the ocean of transformational energy from which everything envisioned emerges.

Here's another example, based on seeking an outlet for our talents. If we don't know who'll require our skills we can throw it open:

> *'Each tree's being is an act of giving,*
> *Yet it plans not how to provide,*
> *It just embraces All-That-Is,*
> *With limbs spread open wide,*
> *I too have natural gifts to give,*
> *And I offer without expectation,*
> *Come now whoever needs my skills,*
> *Step closer with anticipation!'*

All our actions take on extra sparkle when we sing them into being. Our prayer-song may be belted out like a diva or repeated quietly within, like a mantra. It can make worldly sense or be an instinctive crooning. It's the feeling of it – the energetic resonance we evoke – that's important.

Whatever form it takes it's got to have soul.

Lip-Service

Words are just sounds and syllables until they covey our passion and commitment.

Nobody would be touched by a muttered, desultory proclamation of love. Nor one made while we're trying to throttle the object of our supposed affections. Our words, feelings and deeds have to harmonise to make a convincing statement.

It's not possible to bring about lasting change when we're singing our song unenthusiastically, or saying one thing and being another. As an example, John Lennon stood vociferously for peace, and sang his heart out for it, yet still expressed rage at people in his own life. His ex-wife and son were treated with undeserved contempt, his former song-writing partner vilified and he seethed at incompetence in the recording studio. When interviewer Gloria Emerson challenged his authenticity he revealed the vitriol that bubbled below his mellow surface. In my own life I've expressed similar dissonance. Whilst holding a placard with a compassionate message I've yelled abuse at huntsmen as they smugly flouted the fox hunting ban. I became an 'anti', expressing the very aggression I found abhorrent. In so doing I became totally ineffective – I let my Self down.

Indignation about injustice is inescapable but we need to stand *for*, using non-violent direct action to gently, resolutely and *consistently* express empathy and grace.

Who we are – and how we feel – must reveal what we want.

As Ghandi put it '*we have to be the change we want to see in the world*', and be it consciously and completely. Yet we don't have to be perfect. To fight shy of affecting positive change until we're faultless would be like resisting any relationship until we iron out all our personal glitches. *Being the change* is our life's work and an ongoing process; the important thing is to begin it now... tenderly, respectfully and gladly. What we articulate is a vital part of this. In speaking honourably we move towards being the best version of ourselves we can be.

We dance the Dream of Life prayerfully, in awareness.

In the next chapter we'll consider what being aware means.

CHAPTER SIX
Being Awareness

'*The world is profoundly interesting. People are engaging. To find them so, the only requirement is that we be alert and responsive, that we think about what we are seeing and hearing; think beyond ourselves...*'

Jo Coudert

'*There's no separation between the observer and the observed... They're a seamless continuum.*'

J Krishnamurti

'*What is outside me is right inside me, is mine, and vice versa.*'

Novalis

In this chapter we'll consider the second part of our three essential aspects which is *observing*. We'll discuss what wild-spirited observation means and look at how we can observe more effectively in everyday life.

119

Killing It Softly

In 2006 I spent many months housebound through acute illness. During this time I kept positive, thanks to my *unseen* contacts. Yet I missed the stimulation of new encounters in 'the outside world'. I could see my little garden with its attendant starlings but pined for wild nature; for windswept moors and waterfalls and the wheedling cry of great brown buzzards overhead.

When my enforced incarceration finally ended I felt such elation, as vivid now as it was then. At first I only took a few faltering steps down my path, then turned back, but gradually I extended my range to take in the surrounding streets. How amazing I found the world then, even tamed suburbia! Everything was so intense, the greens greener and the scents more evocative than I remembered. The purple passiflora in a neighbour's hedge delighted me with its strange beauty. I marvelled at a delicate yellow poppy, still standing at the roadside in November. What kinship I felt with that resilient little flower! I was always overjoyed to greet somebody I didn't know and share the small wonders of the day with them.

Other people's idea of ordinary had become intensely special to me and I was determined not to lose that sense of awe, even when I saw the sweep of a hill or the rush of a river again.

With patience I built up my range until eventually I was able to book a train journey to take me farther afield. That first foray to the station filled me with astonishment at society's bustle. I felt thrilled by the purposeful activity and the new faces. This excitement continued until I got on the train and found I was the only person in my carriage – and indeed in most carriages – not 'plugged in' to something. Phones, iPods, laptops – all these gadgets necessitated earphones or absorption into a screen. In my fresh, exuberant state this shocked me. There I was prepared for a collective adventure and my travelling companions were doing their best to pretend it wasn't happening! They wanted to pass their time away being preoccupied with another 'reality', deliberately connecting to something only they could hear or see as not to connect directly with the communal experience. It seemed that to them the journey was an inconsequential inconvenience.

It was as if this experience wasn't valid and people were only 'killing time' between more meaningful events.

Despite this disappointment I looked around expectantly as I walked through carriages on my way to the toilet. But people didn't look at me, or each other, unless they were part of a couple or family. And even people travelling together had their own distracting devices with them, locking them into more engrossing worlds of entertainment or work. It seemed there was no conversation unless it was on a phone to an invisible other.

Perhaps they found the Now *dull and would rather replace it with a false construct than address their ennui? Time may not exist, except as a human concept, but actively 'killing it' seemed unwise. It could reinforce an attitude of ingratitude and indifference, even a dangerous disassociation...*

Unable to connect with my fellow passengers, I refused to 'zone out' myself. Instead I decided to focus on what I saw outside the train window. Here are a few of the beautiful moments that the 'plugged in people' around me missed:

- A woman in an orange sari walking down a grubby side street. She looked like a dancing flame in the gloom
- Vibrant graffiti-art sprayed on the railway sidings. One colourful piece read *'hello da people on da train!'*
- An elderly lady filling a wild bird feeder in the yard of a Victorian terraced house
- A sea of golden bracken – a shade I'd never seen that plant turn before – enlivening the monotony of the embankments

121

- The well-established track of a small but determined mammal running up an almost vertical escarpment
- Three ragged children standing in the doorway of a caravan, looking wistfully out across the waste ground on which it stood
- A solitary white-clad walker disappearing across a ploughed field where a flock of birds rose and turned as a single entity

I was so glad I'd seen those fleeting vignettes but sad that nobody else seemed to have shared them. They represented the perfect moments of pleasure human life is composed of. I wanted to shout out *'wake up! You're missing the point of physicality! There'll never be another* Now *like this one!'* but of course I didn't. Instead I fell back into my own pondering.

Train of Thought

I spent the rest of my journey considering what I'd seen through the glass, which prompted me to consider the metaphor of a window.

We habitually put a screen between us and the perceived external – our *non-us* zone. We passively watch simulated reality via computers and televisions or actively engage in an animated, but lifeless, reality through gaming. We see the world once-removed through car windscreens or at a safe distance through the windows of our home. Events aren't experienced as they happen but recorded on camera phones then viewed later on tiny screens or uploaded onto larger ones. We document and share our lives to prove we were there, even though we may as well not have been. This 'life through a lens' establishes an 'inside' and an 'outside' to our experience that reinforces our *forgetting*. Everything's deadened and divided with a screen in-between.

There's no harm in being entertained for relaxation, but not as a means of absenting ourselves. Gadgets are only wonderful when they're supplementary to a life lived in vivid awareness.

When looking out of that train window, I deliberately went against this screening by witnessing myself in all those vignettes. I was simultaneously *out there*, experiencing life in many guises and *in here* as myself, experiencing one perspective. I was *everywhere* in possibility and yet fully present in my apparent individuality.

My challenge was to hold that dual awareness when I stopped observing.

The concept of dual awareness first came to me when I was able to go cycling. Every day I'd ride for miles across the tranquil flat land near my home. This repetitive motion was conducive to a trance-like state and I received insights as I pedalled. On one occasion I suddenly saw everything as whirring particles, like looking at static on an untuned television or a fizzing Seurat painting. *Everything was composed of the same essential energy.* I could only differentiate the cows, grass, fence posts and road around me because of variations in the rate of vibration.

On another occasion I became acutely conscious of 'looking through the windows' of my eyes. I then expected to have a fresh appreciation of my personal viewpoint but instead I became the viewer and the view simultaneously. *The division between what I was seeing and what I was became undetectable.* I was the hand on the handlebar that 'belonged' to my body and I was a passing car, the person driving that car, the blackbird flying low across its path and the bent willow that grew alongside the lane. I was all that I was experiencing...

What I saw was what I was. Whatever I perceived was me.

Yet I wasn't any individual part.

I was everywhere and nowhere.

Because I was witness and witnessed all at once.

I was me, them, you and us...Us. Our Self.

Then I flipped back into my cycling persona of Poppy again,

potentially a much bigger person than I'd been before.

Beside Myself

Whenever I lose sight of the profound simplicity of Oneness – literally – I revisit this 'being outside the box of me' sensation, relating it to the moment I'm in.

1. As I'm doing now: I see my fingers tapping on the keyboard. I stop and stare at them. They're familiar yet curiously intriguing, as if I'm viewing a prospective lover's hands. I observe the crinkled skin, the not entirely clean nails, and the pronounced knuckles in a much more dispassionate way than I'd usually appraise my own body. How strange and marvellous that I can make these things move!

2. But who is the 'I' that makes this movement happen... where is it? When I look at the computer screen before me I appear to be somehow there. When I look back at my hands my focus shifts and with it, my sense of being. Wherever my attention goes it seems 'I' go, too. I'm more fluid, and omnipresent, than I'd previously imagined!

3. Through this realisation, my sense of 'me looking' dissolves away. Now I'm whatever I witness whilst also being somewhere behind, and *beyond*, that witnessing. Amazing! When I let go of the notion of being in my head and 'gazing out' I lose all sense of what I thought I was and instead become whatever I appear to see. *It's all in me and I'm in it.*

4. I explore this sense of *being all things*. Without moving I extend myself to my companion cat curled up by the radiator. Easy for me to believe I'm such a fabulous creature! But now I'm also the fragment of kitchen curtain visible from where I'm sitting. Yes, there's still an 'I' that's sitting: the same 'I' that's seeing. I know this because occasionally it blinks and drags my awareness back to itself . But I'm also over by the window and in every part of the room behind

me. And into the house next door, out through their garden, then down the street to the shop where people queue to be served. Then up above the roof tops, orbiting the Earth and out... My awareness is absolutely *non-local*.

5. Extending my own boundaries and losing a sense of 'small self' like this – actively becoming all I can perceive – is so *beyond* 'ordinary reality' that it can induce both exhilaration and giddiness. It needs practice so I can easily move between each state of awareness, back and forth at will. Now I pull my focus back in. I'm the shadow of my bodily self on my white wall. I'm the hard black frame of this laptop, surrounding the screen on which words magically appear. I'm the hands that type and the sound they make. I'm looking out of the eyes in this body.

6. I'm asking you, the unknown reader: *where are you now? Are you only inside yourself or are you also beside yourself, non-localised yet specific? Will you make this journey to your Self, and back to yourself, with me?*

Do have a play with this. It may not come straight away. There're some days when it's much easier for me than others. But once we've 'got it' we'll want to keep getting it as it changes everything without us doing anything or going anywhere. Like all worthwhile 'spiritual' experiences we can be in solitary confinement, on a mountain top, working in a laundry or relaxing on a Caribbean cruise and we can still be with it – up close and (im)personal.

Are You Local?

The more we can get out of our *localised mind* (the one we believe is exclusively in our own head) and into our *expanded Self* (the one we can experience as being everywhere and nowhere simultaneously) the more likely it is we can behave as engaged, altruistic citizens and not owner-occupiers.

By this I mean we stop being focussed on 'mine' (my children, my home, my job) and broaden out so we feel responsible beyond our possessions. 'Ours' ceases to mean individual property and instead suggests a shared ownership; collective responsibility. So 'their litter' becomes 'our litter' and 'it's not my problem' ceases to be a relevant statement. In this way we feel a genuine, non-sentimental love towards all beings, not just the ones who dwell with us or that bear our genes. This isn't to say we can't feel personal affection, pride or disgust. Our particular human selves, with all their attendant preferences, are part of the dualistic deal. But even as we know our temporary self has likes and dislikes we also understand that we're *bigger* than those things.

As tiny babies, fresh from the Oneness of Infinite Consciousness, we don't experience any difference between 'us' and 'everything else'. As we grow we learn that things are 'me' and 'non-me'. As children this is reinforced and by adolescence it's established fact. As adults we need to learn to switch emphasis from this learned 'little me' back to the 'big me' that encompasses all the other 'me' aspects there are. We can then hold both 'little and 'big' aspects in balance, shifting our awareness back and forth at will.

Then we can look around a train carriage full of individuals, and know we're the unique witness but also the people, the carriage and everything outside the train.

And even if the carriage is full of distracted folk who couldn't care less what we're doing, or thinking – or even that we exist at all – it still applies.

After that initial train journey I wondered if travelling had always been like that, so detached and insular? Had I just forgotten? Or had things somehow deteriorated in my absence from public life? If it was the former then clearly I'd been guilty of zoning out behaviour or it would've struck me as odd before.

126

Whichever, I was grateful my eyes had been opened. I'd no longer collude in this non-experience; this collective avoidance of life.

I hope you'll feel the same way upon sharing this with me.

Tuning Back in

Of course, other people are committed to helping us re-engage.

Sound artist Bill Montana works with ambient sounds of the city – the everyday music of the streets – and makes people hear the mundane in a different way. He allows ambient noise to be more than a background buzz to be tuned out until the next important thing happens. It becomes a symphony of which we – with our footsteps and breath – are a part. Montana counterpoints this urban music with the sounds of the sea, making the parallel between what we consider to be meaningful and what we filter out as interference.

I frequently see people wearing headphones outdoors, even in green places filled with birdsong and interesting natural interactions. Not just teens but dog walkers, postal workers... anyone. Similarly people routinely walk along texting or talking on the phone. They don't see each other or the world. They're going somewhere and it's the somewhere that's important, not the journey filled with the incidental music of life.

Yet as anyone on a spiritual quest knows, it's the journey that matters.

It's an insult to treat our life experiences in such a throwaway manner. As if most of our days are filled with pointless spaces to be filled by distraction until we're ready to re-enter the 'safe' or 'valid' world of colleagues/friends/family. Just as a cat will deliberately filter all subsidiary sounds, only paying attention to the ones that directly concern it, so humanity's learning how to obliterate 'unnecessary' people, places and events. People are deliberately disconnecting from unpredictable 'ordinary reality' and connecting to a clean and controllable version.

The volume's being turned down on life; on the richness of this shared Now.

If we routinely absent ourselves and practice avoidance we'll become oblivious to the intricate interplay of light/sound/ colour/form that makes up the apparent world. Eventually we'll become incapable of responding to whatever arises outside of our artificial comfort zone.

Let's challenge this with our own behaviour.

One of the ways we can deliberately reconnect, or tune ourselves back in, is by using the technique known as *mindfulness*. The teacher Eckhart Tolle refrains from using this much-coined Buddhist term as it suggests *mind-fullness*. This is because of the Western translation, not the Buddha's intent, but still this term isn't sufficient to describe the awareness – or alert presence – we wish to express. Author William Bloom prefers *kindfulness*: being awake, connected and living. As we're aiming to unite the seen and *unseen* aspects of being I prefer the term *soulfulness* – being fully in our empathetic eternal aspect as we live in the physical world.

Generally when we say 'I' we point to our heart, not our head. Similarly when we say something has affected us deeply – soul-deep – we'd thump our chest, not tap our skull. Our soul isn't located anywhere physical – it's non-local, beyond the body – but paradoxically it's at our responsive core...at the heart of us. Soulfulness isn't about thinking but *being*. When we're soulful we act on our highest impulse. We don't need to work out what's best; we *know*, but that knowing isn't thought-based. Meditation, or *entering the silence*, is the tool that connects us to this soulful – considerately thoughtless, not thought-full – state. Hopefully by now we're well used to *entering the silence* and enjoying its benefits. Yet we can also bring soulfulness into our daily lives moment-by-moment, through observing. Like now.

All Together Now

What's actually going on in this moment we're sharing?

Firstly we're both reading the same words. I, at my keyboard, you with the printed page before you. I can sense you; can you sense me? What about all the others who may be reading this page concurrently? Or those who've read, and will read, these words?

Be aware of me, and of them, as I'm aware of you. And then be aware of all else. All those who are eating and sleeping and walking...on and on, out from where we're sitting reading to the next room, house, road, town, county, country...

There's no past or future, only this eternal unfolding *Now.* We're connecting by focussing on one action, one moment – one energetic reality.

One. Oneness.

Now bring your attention back in to yourself. There're physical things that're happening to us both. For me I can feel the sciatic pain gnawing at my left buttock and hear my companion cat snoring as the wind whistles outside. My hand goes to my mouth; my lips are dry. I sigh; wiggle my toes in my slippers. The other cat gets up and walks to the kitchen, where I realise my tap is still dripping. I sense my irritation, both at needing to repair the tap and at my cat's wanting more food. Then I become aware that my irritation doesn't matter. I smile and will get up now, to stroke him, for he is another me, just as you are. I'm aware of you, as you're reading this. What are you feeling and doing? I greet you silently, in my soul, not my mind. It's such a privilege to share this experience with you.

Us, fully present together. Soulfully.

Well, I enjoyed that brief foray, let's do it more often! But is it practical? Soulfulness is all very well when we're writing/reading this book, but how do we sustain it? How to maintain soulfulness in a fast world that demands attention but gains only our superficial awareness, cluttered with extraneous thoughts?

Essential Maintenance

There are three ways in which we can practice soulfulness, using our observational skills:

- *Being a witness*
- *Being a sensualist*
- *Being a good listener*

All three centre on our being *vitally present* – alive to the moment.

1. *The witness* observes from their eternal standpoint, rather than experiencing only from their human one. This witnessing self isn't remote, but rather compassionate in its detachment. Detachment is a loving *non-attachment* to our human condition and its attendant struggles as we know them to be transient. The paradox is *we care but we don't care* – we appreciate something matters whilst knowing in the greater scheme of things that it doesn't.

   Pain is a great tool for practicing witnessing. It gives us an opportunity to separate our true eternal selves out from temporary bodily sensations. Pain isn't us and it's not really ours, as nothing belongs to us except for our unique awareness. It's just another sensory experience like heat or moisture, only this sensation can't be shared, like feeling rain can. We all know when something hurts but can never know what someone else is feeling; just as we can't know how anybody else tastes a banana, only that they do. Pain provides a unique learning experience; a chance to gauge our endurance and understand what it means to us. When we don't need to blank out the pain to get on with other things we can be with it and see what it's telling us.

Disown pain and it becomes interesting, not overwhelming. Then we can observe it as we would a compelling but disturbing painting.

Whereas the witness is responding from its eternal position and observing physicality, the sensualist indulges fully in physicality whilst knowing it's all illusory... a sensuous dream. They're opposite approaches but equally valid and ultimately integrated.

2. *Sensualism* was first introduced to me when I was experiencing extreme anxiety. This anxiety began after I was injected with the wrong dose of pain medication by a doctor and left alone in a dark room, struggling not to leave my manifest body. I wasn't able to call for help or move and all my focus was on keeping body and soul together. When the effects of the drug eventually wore off I was left in a highly 'jangled' state, my body burned out with adrenaline. I began having panic attacks one after the other. If I tried to fall asleep they'd wake me. After six weeks of being unable to take solid food or get any rest I had to seek help.

   Part of this help was a technique to keep me grounded in my environs, not distracted by anxiety. I had to act as if I was a newcomer to Earth and encounter the things around me afresh, using all my senses. I had to stroke, grip and rub whatever came to hand: the upholstery of my seat, the linen on my bed, the wood of the door, the crinkly faux leather of my bag. The texture of objects previously taken for granted became a source of wonder. I let descriptive words for these texture sensations fill my thoughts: *nubbly, grainy, fuzzy*. I closed my eyes and let myself 'see' the fabric I was touching. Then I'd open my eyes and look with all the concentration of a child marvelling at a palm full of sand on a beach. Everything I studied became a tiny new world of hues, shadows and imperfections.

My senses were similarly captivated by scent. When I was still in the acute phase of my panicking I kept some pungent items around me: rosemary essential oil, damp earth, musty old wood, vinegar. I also sought out the subtler aromas of things that would ordinarily be considered scentless: paint on a wall, a cup, a cardboard box. There was always a faint tang that told a story, however slight.

And if I employed touch, sight and smell all at once then objects became almost incredible; worlds unto themselves.

The poet Antony Gormley suggests we can become sensualists by walking barefoot from March to November. By this we learn a whole new vocabulary of sensation through our sensitive soles. Gormley says this is also a way of showing solidarity with those who don't wear shoes and a renewed respect for, and awareness of, the land in which we live. As our feet caress the ground the world reveals itself in far more detail than before.

3. *Good listening* was briefly mentioned in the previous chapter as being important. I maintain that basic counselling skills are essential to every human, as central to counselling are the art of listening and the development of empathy. Get into the habit of observing conversations. Does the listener maintain eye contact with the speaker, making them feel that what they're saying is the most important thing that's happening? Do they give other signals that they're paying attention, nodding or making encouraging sounds? Do they allow the speaker to finish before coming back with a response, taking time to digest what's been said first? Do they seem to observe as well as listening, picking up what's *not* being said out loud by the communicator?

Do they stay with the experience and enjoy it, or does attention wander?

It's soon easy to spot what's real listening and what's a superficial batting about of language to score points. Real listening makes a tangible connection – a circuit. The more we give our full attention, the more the focus of our attention will give us. And the more we look the more we'll see – of ourselves as well as the apparent 'other'. When we give one hundred percent of our awareness to an everyday exchange, we both have a more soul-full experience.

We'll *be the love*, which is what we'll focus on next.

CHAPTER SEVEN
Please Live Generously

'Whatever we admire, so are we. Whatever we reject, so are we. Whatever we perceive is what we are. And what we are is All-That-Is.'

From Inner Guidance

'While there's a lower class, I am it; while there's a criminal element, I am of it; while there's a soul in prison, I am not free.'

Eugene V. Debs

'My love of life is total. Everything I do is an expression of that love. Everything I write is a love song.'

Penny Rimbaud

'...It's so easy to hate; it takes strength to be gentle and kind.'

Morrissey

In this penultimate chapter we'll look at the third of our trio of essential aspects: *loving*. We'll consider what loving means and rediscover what it is to love unconditionally, *without exception*. This, beyond all other aspects, is our real wild-spirited challenge.

Love Story

We've come to understand, through sharing ideas and through our own reconnection to All-That-Is, that there are many questions but only one real answer: *empathy*. Empathy is true, guileless tenderness that knows no bounds. It's love in fluid action – true altruistic love, not a romantic fervour based in our needs.

As we've previously considered, dramatic fiction expands our empathy as it allows us to effortlessly experience life from many viewpoints. In a good story, characters seem to exist and a believable reality is created around them. The author holds all this within them before gifting it to the world. Similarly the Wild Dreamer holds all potential individuals and life-stories within Itself before they appear to unfold as our personal life-drama. By this we can think of our own manifest existence as a narrative we may learn empathy by. Our tale has central themes and protagonists but also peripheral characters and story lines we're barely aware of. These fringe aspects weave in seamlessly, supporting and augmenting our plot. Similarly we support other people's plots even though we've never encountered them.

How does this work?

A man is late for work after being kept awake by his inconsiderate noisy neighbour. In his haste he drops his wallet. The single mother who finds it does what most of us would do, she checks for the cash inside. She sees it's enough to buy her and their children food for a week. Tempted but unsure, she takes it to a café and ponders on what to do. Surely she could take the loose change to buy herself a snack? As she goes to the counter she overhears a conversation about the devastating effect of a burglary on an elderly couple. Feeling uncomfortable she leaves and takes the wallet untouched to the Police station. While she's sitting waiting to fill in a form an electrician who's been working in the building comes through the reception area. They used to go to school together. He always liked her and now asks her to go out with him at the weekend...amazing how they never bumped into each other before!

And so the love story goes on. The man with the wallet is part of it yet they'll never know how returning his intact wallet restored his faith in humanity and changed his own responses. And he'll never know their tale.

Similarly, think of a mouthful of food on the way to our lips. We're the end of its story. But where's its beginning? Trace the food's journey back through the people involved – the supermarket checkout, the shelf stacker, the delivery driver, the packer, the picker, the grower – and each of their tales touches ours. None of them knows us but we're part of their story and of the land where the food grew.

However, while we appear to have a story that intertwines we also know – and here's that dual awareness again – that we've no story. That's why they're life *stories*, not life facts. Our individual experience – our person-ality – is a fiction: a wild dream. We're the Wild Dreamer that contains all characters/tales but isn't really any of them.

Method Acting

We're all our Wild Dreaming Self can hold within It. We're:
- *The arthritic sweatshop worker bent over a machine*
- *The bear fretting fiercely in captivity*
- *The ant carrying a leaf across the forest floor*
- *The elderly priest giving the sacrament*
- *The bluebottle buzzing against the windowpane*
- *The business tycoon in his chartered plane*
- *The convicted murderer learning to read*
- *The hawk swooping to snatch an ailing vole*
- *The tribal elder teaching voodoo to her grandson*
- *The teenage addict cuddling her second child*
- *The gazelle brought down kicking in the dust*
- *The gaping fish writhing on the trawler's deck*

137

- *The pulsar star as it spins like a dervish*
- *The sniper coolly taking aim to fire*
- *The ballet dancer pirouetting for the first time*
- *The cobra arching to strike again*
- *The person who printed this page*

There're bound to be some characters in that list that we identify with and others we instinctively recoil from, unable to relate to who or what they are. Yet those we don't warm to are all in our Self – they're other parts of Us. We can't reject them outright as that'd be dishonest. What we can say is they're just aspects of our Being we don't understand so well. We recognise their validity as part of a cohesive whole but don't choose to express those qualities as individual beings. They're Us, but not *us*.

With this understanding, we can accept we all have the capability to behave like Myra Hindley, Pol Pot or Heimlich Himmler as well as Nelson Mandela or Frances Power Cobbe. They're in Us, and so in us too – experienced personally as extremes of aggression and resentment or dependability and tenderness. Most of us lie somewhere between the extremes of cruelty and virtue. We own and acknowledge the whole spectrum of emotional expressions within us but don't necessarily act upon them all. Generally we choose not to express the spite that may be gratifying at the time but leaves us feeling disgusted and remorseful. Yet most of us have to try out our capability for cruelty at least once to see that we don't like its effects. We have to find out *how not to be* for our generosity and consideration to have true meaning.

To *be the love* we must accept our potential for being the opposite. We need also examine why most of us remain mediocre when we could be honourable role-models in our own life-drama.

Uncomfortably Numb

The little boy who hits the smaller, less quick lad will hopefully grow to regret tormenting another human being. However, the boy who pulls the wings off flies or sets fire to ants may not grow up to feel the same way about tormenting his fellow creatures. This is because the society he lives in has ascribed a hierarchy to living beings: certain races or types of humanity over others, followed by other mammals, birds, reptiles, fish and insects. Sentience – and possibly a soul – can be ascribed arbitrarily to any of these, depending on culture or creed. Or, indeed, to none of them.

Usually we give en-souled status to those creatures most like us – *'oh, they're so human!'* – followed by companion animals. Consequently primates subject to abuse elicit the most compassionate response, followed by horses, cats and dogs. The bigger the mammal is (having a greater mental capacity) the more we allow for it being conscious, ascribing the brain to the seat of awareness/feeling. However, we continue to call large farmed mammals 'poor dumb creatures' thus establishing their convenient exemption from this rule. Then there're small furry creatures, cute but negated by wont of brain size. Also they're often considered pests and pests can't be aware as that'd be too inconvenient for us. Birds are admired but their obvious cranial deficit – and their complete difference from us – is equated to being insensate. The same goes for fish, as they're even less comprehensible...plus some taste good and we can't ascribe responsiveness to those we want to eat. Amphibians are cold blooded and therefore cold-hearted. Pretty, useful insects such as bees and butterflies are respected but we see their stature as reflecting their spiritual content. Other insects are seen as creepy nuisances. Those that hurt or scare us – the sharks and wasps of our earlier analogy, along with snakes, spiders, scorpions, fleas – are as alien races to us. They look strange, behave unpredictably, don't serve us and may even be out to get us. In short, they're *other* than us.

When a creature is deemed *other* it's often *desentientised* – credited as having lesser, or no, awareness. A being that isn't sentient has no sensitivity – it's *desensitised* – and so we needn't be concerned with its welfare. It becomes okay to use them, treating them as we would any other inanimate object. The Nazis applied this logic to the mentally/physically disabled, then the Jews, Roma, homosexuals, etc.

When we desensitise the victim we're also anaesthetising part of our own being. Instead of making us more powerful or superior – 'more than' – it always makes us the 'less than' we dislike, or more likely, fear...less responsive, less imaginative and less considerate.

Once we've learned how to conveniently compartmentalise the *other* it's easier to justify more reductive delineations and so cut off more aspects of our self, making us partially numb. In this partially deadened state we act in a disorientated, disassociated way. Thus animal abusers often end up as abusers of other humans, especially children or vulnerable adults. We may react with a fervent '*I'm not like that*' but with a little honest examination we'll find that we've created some form of segregation within ourselves. We may've ascribed *otherness* to members of different cultures, religions, professions, sexual preferences, social habits or even supporters of another football team to ours – and probably to members other species.

Of course it's fine to have light-hearted predilections. Individual experience is all about choices. But preferences shouldn't become prejudices, devaluing any that fall outside the prescribed boundary of our personal tastes.

We may not like all the characters in a book but we know they have a purpose and so accept them. By applying this acceptance to our own life stories we can understand that there are no others, only another self – a self that's apparently different to us but fulfilling an equally valid role...whether we like it or not.

We'll need to go deep to identify the areas of our being that we've anaesthetised so profoundly we're not consciously aware of them. Our *unseen* companions can help with this process. Only when we've undertaken a full and fearless internal inventory of our ingrained bigotry can we reunite all aspects of our Self within ourselves and become an effective whole again.

We can't be the love when part of us is engaged in suppressing Itself. We can only be the love when we're open to being each other, without conditions.

Of course whatever applies to us personally applies externally, in society. Any system based solely on humanity's values/ preferences needs to be reassessed. Until every being's sentience and innate sensitivity are acknowledged and respected we'll always be fragmented.

One day we'll find our species-ism and human-centricity as abhorrent as racism. We'll also find the killing our own kind unacceptable, because we're one another, not an other.

Not in My Name

The most primary calculation of wild spirituality is:

Every one equals One.

Either this is true or it isn't. We can't attach convenient sub-clauses.

If we accept this, yet choose to act contrary to it, then this is the only real wrongdoing. To know we're doing wrong *is* wrong. All other things we do without knowing are mistakes to be learned from.

For a wild spirit to condone, or actually take, another self's life – for whatever reason – is perverse. It's suicide as well as homicide.

I currently live in a town so near to a military area that my crockery rattles when they're running shelling exercises. Although my neighbours seem to accept this din as easily as the cheering from a local football match, I can't. I understand that for the most part the military personnel are pleasant individuals who just enjoy the active life and camaraderie. I realise without the military they may be directionless, perhaps even destitute. And I know they're not *other*. However, I think their choice is abhorrent – the opposite of *being the love* – and I won't normalise what they do.

Tolerating any aspect of war, be that prospective or operational, isn't possible when we remember we're One. When we attack another self the Self always suffers – there can be no winners.

War is about many things but primarily insecurity, intolerance and greed, all mainstays of the *forgetting*. The more *forgetful* a chief, group or nation is the more likely they'll overcompensate for their uncertainty. Lacking spiritual orientation they'll strive to expand their material possessions and territory, seeking confirmation of their personal, and national, supremacy. It's fine to enjoy the traditions/achievements of a state or culture, just as we enjoy our own individual traits. But an understanding of our essential Oneness – our *remembering* – should be kept as a counterpoint to any such acknowledgment or celebration. With this dual awareness, jingoism – or proclaiming ultimate superiority – are absurd at best and a travesty at worst. When we *remember* there's no need to prove or defend anything. Having our homeland or national behaviour insulted isn't the end of the world, because there is no world...not really.

We realise it's all illusory – a playful game; a life-story...a love story. Or it should be, because the only thing that abides is our essential unity and the mutual caring born of it.

Inevitably when we challenge the validity of war the same point is raised – *'what do we do if a Hitler attacks? Shouldn't we defend what's right?'*

Clearly prevention is better than aggressive cure. There'll always be rogue – or cancerous – cells in any collective, as there is in an individual body. The difference is whether we give them an environment to grow unimpeded or not. In our current self-centred, compartmentalised and stressed society it's possible to become downtrodden, isolated and neglected. An unbalanced soul – or a sensitive person who's already become overloaded by electro-magnetic/chemical toxicity – may not have the strength to overcome these hardships, becoming intolerant, embittered or confused. They may then amalgamate with other disturbed *forgetful* elements and become inflamed. As with cancer we spot these enraged conglomerations too late and deal with them brutally, meeting force with force. We react with surprised outrage, as if this was an unexpected invasion and not part of our Self revealing an integral (and really rather obvious) problem. We provide the breeding ground but never expect the inevitable results. We expend vast amounts of energy – and money – in a blatant foot-stamping display of deterrence when the simple restorative grace of the *remembering* is ours for free.

Instead of reacting to every new flare up we need a nurturing, inclusive approach – not an overtly competitive one. When we emerge as newborns into this reality we should be assured of our role as vital cells in the body of Creation, no better and no worse than any other. We should be brought up *remembering* our parity; empowered together by truth, not encouraged to *forget*. Then a rogue element would stand out as impotent and ridiculous. A Hitler figure couldn't be the menace of nations without other uneasy, befuddled individuals joining his separatist delusion. No cell would amalgamate with them, yet they'd not be ostracised. Rather than being attacked or outlawed they'd be recognised for what they are: *a version of our Self, expressing aspects of being that we ourselves choose not to express.* They wouldn't be invalidated, to be eradicated, but learned from. They'd be supported in their recovery, according to how we'd wish to be treated ourselves.

In a state of *remembering* we'd encourage *interdependent individuality*, not establish a bland or rigid conformity. Misunderstandings would be good-natured but meaningful debates, not declarations of war. There'd be nothing to fight but everything – All Possibility – to tenderly explore. Creative coexistence would be the norm and peace naturally proliferate.

Hopelessly naive? No, hopefully naive. The sophisticated lie we're used to is hard to maintain, requiring ever more complex ruses. The truth, and how to live it, is so simple.

So simple that I know that killing my kin – kin of whatever

143

species or stripe – is inherently wrong. It's not *being the love*. I can't smile indulgently as the tanks pass through town. I can't support self-harm and the destruction of what I hold dear. I don't have to engage in a battle to know that no matter how it may appear we're always dropping bombs *on us*.

There's no outside, no inside; no sides at all. And no exceptions.

It's brave to accept that there's no enemy but our self. The men in the trenches discovered this when they met their supposed adversaries to play football on Christmas Day 1914. Not only was their nemesis just like them, *they were them*. Them in other circumstances, with other accents and customs, but them just the same – beings that laughed, cried and bled. Boundless, borderless beings whose souls flew home when their temporary bodies fell. But for a few props in the theatre of war there was no difference.

There never is.

Vengeance Isn't Mine

Although we need to establish a society based on *remembering* what do we do meanwhile when faced with crimes against ourselves?

How we can allow hurt to any another being – human or non-human – and not want to stop it by any means possible?

This must be one of the hardest issues for the wild-spirited human to face. Surely it's right to hurt in order to prevent somebody hurting? No, it isn't. *Not ever*. Because by adding more harm into the equation we're perpetuating a cycle; establishing an undesirable precedent. Hating the hateful damages us – all of us – more than it does the recipient. This retribution may be temporarily satisfying for our human selves but it's utterly dismaying for our eternal aspect. '*An eye for an eye will make the whole world blind*,' as Ghandi famously said.

Yet beyond the well-meaning rhetoric can we *be the love* when faced with the polar opposite? Is it ridiculously unrealistic? If we're to keep faith with our selves and retain any integrity then we have to try – and keep trying – to prevent cruelty by non-violent direct means. *Because hate can only ever be overcome by love.* Certainly we can live compassionately as a matter of course, directing our attention – and so our energy – unwaveringly to the good. Living cruelty-free and being kind, in both thought and deed, is an ongoing act of love. But we can also stand in harm's way because we don't fear the consequences.

We're eternal beings and so physical hardship, even endings, are irrelevant.

Not that we court danger or death, but we can put ourselves between the aggressor and the victim if needs be.

Here's an example of this love in action. Peace Pilgrim walked tirelessly across the United States, Canada, Mexico, Alaska and Hawaii between 1953 until her death in 1981. She knew the message of peace and not the messenger (herself) to be important: *she was Peace, literally.* On her endless travels she witnessed an eight year old girl being chased into a barn by a man. Following, Peace saw the man keep coming at the girl who was now cowering in a corner. Peace was by this time an elderly lady but she still fearlessly put her body between the man and the girl. As she said, '*I just stood and looked at this poor, psychologically sick man with loving compassion.*' The man stopped approaching and looked at her for a while, then turned and walked away. Not a word was spoken but Peace had calmly communicated to the eternal wise aspect of that man and it'd responded.

Such non-violent direct intervention is utterly fearless and centred in acceptance of Infinite Consciousness. As Peace herself said '*if we can remember we're not really separate from each other it may increase our wish to transform rather than subdue.*' We've become used to the quick-fix of self-satisfaction that base-level reactions give us but resolute gentleness brings the long-lasting change we want to see.

We must be the love. Persistently and faithfully. Not just when faced with the big injustices but when faced with the small details of life that perpetuate division and therefore abuse.

But how else can we *be the love*, in practical terms?

We Love Us

Firstly let's look at what we consider to be a loving gesture.

Obviously all beneficent acts are intrinsically valuable. Yet often they're fuelled by personal motivation or identification which means they're finite and boundaried, not free-flowing. For example, we support the breast cancer charity because we've a family member who perished of the disease. We buy a decent birthday present for our friend because we'd like one in return. We work for underprivileged children because we've a child and wouldn't want them to suffer similar indignities. We give food to the local animal shelter because we love our terriers. We pass a compliment because we want the woman to think well of us and hopefully reciprocate. We volunteer to drive Alzheimer's patients because our father has the onset of dementia and we fear we may one day have it too.

Wild spirituality encourages us to move beyond these individual incentives to a genuinely altruistic way that isn't about recognition or ownership.

Real love requires no reason or reward:

- *It's not because we both belong to the same culture/ethnicity*
- *It's not because we feel sorry for, or protective of, someone due to their age*
- *It's nothing to do with physical looks; whether we find someone attractive*
- *It's not because we share religious affiliations/belief systems*
- *Or because our religion requires good deeds from us*
- *It's not related to an admiration of abilities/achievements*
- *It's not because someone's 'safe', 'trusted' or 'acceptable' to us*
- *It's not because someone pleased us, or because we want them to*

In fact we don't even enter into a loving engagement. It's

beyond 'I' and 'you'.

It's just because we *remember* who we all are – all of us – and want to express that understanding with gratitude and pleasure.

Similarly, *I love you* doesn't need to be the reassuring, possessive, romantic or sentimental statement it's become.

Instead it simply and generously states:

'You're valued and respected as my kin beyond the skin. I recognise your worth as another cell in the body of Creation. We're superficial strangers but deeply connected – we're both the Creator and so we're each other. There's no separation and no expectation. We are; so love is.'

When we take this as our mantra our generosity can be enduring; endless. It's fuelled by the highest, deepest, widest good and so is a bottomless resource, not dependent on anything but our being present.

The nearest people have got to spontaneously feeling this without *remembering* is during a near-death experience (N.D.E). Often they report the Infinitely Conscious experience of being everywhere and nowhere, but also being in, or with, the most overwhelming love. For example, teenager Ben Breedlove recently made a video of himself describing his previous, gloriously love-filled N.D.Es before he finally died of his heart condition. Yet Infinite Consciousness isn't about love as such but rather *absolute regard for any and all aspects of Itself.* Acknowledgment and appreciation are expressed for each facet of being, regardless of its type. Our Self doesn't have human preferences, or indeed any preferences. Therefore the wonderful feeling people recall from an N.D.E isn't love but *unconditional acceptance.* It's taken for love as that's the closest human emotion we've got to such an unreservedly munificent, accommodating response.

We don't need an N.D.E to know how to relate like this because it's in our essential nature. The more we reconnect with our Self by *entering the silence* the more we're *being the love*, bringing that appreciative energy into 'ordinary reality' with us.

But how do we express it in society?

Public Acts of Love

Though we may feel clumsy and embarrassed at first, the more we show unconditional regard the easier it gets. It's just a habit we've lost but can deliberately find again.

If an overt display seems a step too far we can start off by expressing it covertly. I racked my brains to think of effective ways to do this but while I was only applying my mind, there was no clarity. The instant I applied my wild soul to the problem and engaged my *unseen* companions, I was presented with an answer swiftly...

You love words and know their power? Then say I love you *through public art.*

I'd recently seen a skilfully stencilled image on the side of a derelict pub, thoughtfully – in fact lovingly – positioned where people regularly have to sit in traffic jams. It was of an unremarkable man accompanied with the words '*imagination gives you wings to fly*'. I was moved by the artist's need to inspire and entertain those trapped in their cars, without taking credit. It was a selfless act of beauty – of genuine love – with no ego involved. How refreshing!

On seeing this I wondered what it'd be like to engage in such an act. The notion of spray-painting put me off as there were implications in using a toxic substance and disposing of the can afterwards. Also it needed time to execute it well and I wasn't fit enough to run away if challenged! I knew there must be another gentle, whimsical way to put *I love you* out there. Perhaps in colourful chalk in the manner of pavement artists, something that washed away in the rain? Or better, by quickly putting up beautiful ready-made posters with flour and water paste.

Posters that weren't selling anything or targeting – or alienating – anyone.

People would see these multiplying *I love you* messages in their urban spaces and at least raise a smile. Perhaps they'd think it was a message of one romantic partner to another, or from a parent to a child. Whatever their immediate thoughts the impression would be good: it's a generous non-threatening message. And as the statement was anonymous there'd be nobody to be suspicious of because of their age, sex, race or general physicality. There'd be nothing to take offence over.

Maybe if the posters kept appearing everywhere, passers-by would realise the message of love wasn't intended for a specific person. Then for who? For them? Why not? How wonderful to be cherished when we're feeling stressed, low; disconnected. *I love you!* Who loves us? It wouldn't matter.

We're loved.

We'd remember this at times of stress. We'd begin to act as if it were true, holding our head up. We'd feel valued and start to act accordingly. It'd make us feel so good that we'd want to make other people feel good too. So we'd start putting the message out ourselves. Why not? What's there to lose? It's free and easy.

- *It's written in rainbow hues on a slip of paper in a library book*
- *It's stamped on envelopes we receive through the post*
- *It's printed on homemade badges left on bus seats*
- *There're stickers on items we pick up in the supermarket*
- *And there it is again displayed in the windows of houses*

The 'random acts of love' just keep coming.

So we start putting this bold, bright message in greetings cards and send them to people we don't know: neighbours, local shop assistants, attendants at the leisure centre, teachers, nurses, carers, local politicians...anyone. Why not? They may be suspicious and throw the card away, or dismiss it as embarrassing or silly, but there're others who'll feel touched and treasured and they'll pass the idea on themselves.

Love's infectious and we're the carrier. People's responses aren't our responsibility. Like the Universe we just keep expanding our embrace. There can never be too much of a good thing.

And what if we went outside the peopled areas and created collaborative art with the spirit of a wild place? Then *I love you* could be expressed in as many different ways as the land inspired:

- *Spelled out in chalk and flint on a downland hillside*
- *Picked out in driftwood and pebbles on the beach*
- *Carved into the earth with a stick in a woodland clearing*

As with a crop circle, the human maker would be irrelevant; the only meaning being derived from the pleasure it gave the viewer and its own graceful symmetry *in situ*. Like sand art that washes or blows away it'd be pristine and perfect while it lasted. Nothing would be artificially manufactured and nothing destroyed, only temporarily rearranged. The message would linger long after the organic reminder had gone, its meaning absorbed and transmuted by the stones, seeds, trees, birds and on. As with Dr. Masaru Emoto's experiments regarding the transformative energy of kind words on water crystals, we'd transfer the vibration of our language deep into the earth itself.

Photos of this art could be taken, collated and shared on blogs or Facebook. It'd be wonderful if, in Internet terms, the love infection would 'go viral'.

I've begun by spelling out *I love you* in chalk on my local hills. It's a laborious process but worth it. The first time I found someone else had written it too I was moved to tears. One day I – or perhaps we – will write it so big that those passing below on the road can read it, feel it and be it. One day I'll be creating marvellous, affecting statements as yet undreamed of. Because I'm Infinite Consciousness and endlessly resourceful.

And so are you.

I love you!

Walking the Talk

I wondered how it'd be to communicate Oneness by walking around with *I love you* emblazoned on a t-shirt or jacket. What stir would it cause; what discomfiture? Would people ridicule, be intrigued or turn away in embarrassment? One thing was for sure – I'd need absolute conviction the message, no matter what response it garnered.

I love you when you mock; I love you when you turn away, even when you attack.

The crowded British Isles can be a fragmented, distrustful place with little that appears to unite us. Could one uncharismatic middle-aged woman touch any hearts? Should she even bother?

Yes, because the little 'she' doesn't matter. 'She' is transient. 'She' is just one expression of the One which sustains. And gently reminds...

We are not the issue. It's our honest desire to promote the *remembering* that's important. The outcome isn't our business. How can we know what our actions will lead to in a day, a month, a year after we've gone? Whether we undertake a pilgrimage or peace across a continent on foot, or write a letter of support to someone suffering, it's the motivation – the energetic impetus – behind the act that's valuable. Doing small things with a genuinely loving intent is just as valid as the grander gestures.

It's carefully filling in the detail that gives depth to the bigger picture.

Wouldn't it be wonderful if there were so many of us routinely walking around our towns and villages with *I love you* emblazoned upon our clothing that it became acknowledged, even welcomed?

Ah, here comes one of those nice love people to remind me of who I am and what's important right now.

Better still, what if we told people we loved them as naturally as we say 'good morning'? What if *I love you* became our common greeting? Being introduced to someone would be just like that old song by The Doors...

'Hello, I love you; won't you tell me your name?'

Of course, mystics and sages have been expressing love for millennia through parables, psalms and poetry. They realised they were Infinite Consciousness having a human experience and wanted to celebrate that fact. Not to evangelise for the sake of converting people but to bring others back to the wonder of their Self. We're just reiterating their age old message in the broadest, yet most intimate, sense. The repetition in as many forms as we can imagine it allows *I love you* to become habitual; natural. Who among us could say, hand on heart, that we've reached a level of understanding that requires no further prompting? Surely even if our societies were flourishing and centred in truth, creativity and empathy we'd still wish to hear those three magic words? Magic because they invoke the highest condition and so transcend 'ordinary' reality, even as they penetrate it deeply.

Love should flow like water because it's as essential as water to life. Let's all be a conduit to the flow, not another obstacle.

Pouring Our Heart Out

Here are some more simple suggestions for *being the love*:

1. *Treat a creature or insect we can't relate to, or are afraid of, with loving respect as an equal.*
2. *Respond lovingly to a public figure previously designated as 'the enemy'.* Be kind to their errors of judgement, made in public, and so to our own faults.
3. *Stroke, or sing to, a plant that doesn't 'belong' to us; reminding ourselves they're in our care, not our property.* All creation is autonomous, even in its vulnerability.
4. *Forgive someone we know – a relative we believe hurt us, a friend we think wronged us, even a local paedophile.* In doing so we forgive ourselves for the thing we say we'll never forgive our self for.
5. *Write to a prisoner on Death Row in the USA through the UK organisation* Lifelines. Their mistakes may be more drastic than ours, but we all make mistakes. And we all need love, especially when facing such a torturous sentence.
6. *Remember the 'unknown dead' – the human and non-human victims of wars, persecutions, neglect, disease and abuse.* Because we do know them: *they're us.*
7. *Acknowledge the pain of the 'unknown living' – including those suffering through their own actions, like addicts.* Or those suffering through inflicting suffering on others, like

murderers. Because the more hurt we inflict, the more hurt we become ourselves...and the more love we need.

8. *Give love to a captive creature, like a dairy cow.* This may seem a poor substitute for releasing them but setting them free may cause more harm than good. Don't turn away in disempowered shame but *towards*, showing these forgotten beings the love they so richly deserve in their limited lifetime.

9. *Greet a 'stranger' as a friend – in the supermarket, at the garage, in the street... everywhere!* This can be the most difficult gesture of all, as it's often returned with incomprehension or hostility. But smiling is about being bigger than our small self with all its attendant fears. *It's not about us; it's about Us.* Together, with perseverance, we can make suspicious separatism a thing of the misguided past and love our shared *modus operandi*.

So why are these gestures more than being ethical or just plain nice? Our unassailable connection to Oneness makes all the difference. It empowers and inspires our actions, making them resonate through the realms and so be felt more deeply. Likewise our *unseen* companions help our energies to be disseminated throughout their levels of existence, including the fabulous worlds of Faery. With such a profound connection, and with such excellent support, what once took effort becomes as natural as the next breath...and as enlivening. The loving impetus of our gestures flows past any temporary fear or awkwardness; through any personal desire or need. It comes from a wild, spontaneous place beyond what we think, she thinks or they think. Indeed beyond thought – especially any thought of recompense – as such love can't be rationalised.

It just is; an earthly, yet eternal, expression of Oneness.

When we know our true appreciative nature it's impossible not to express it, unfailingly. It's a matter of the deep green heart – of the unconditionally accepting Self. That's my priority, and I hope it's yours too.

Because that's what's everlastingly ours, beyond any reasonable doubt.

CHAPTER EIGHT
Baggage Check-In

*'How do I work within – and live happily and joyfully within –
a society that's completely crazy and doing bonkers things...
And not get caught up in it?'*

Leo Rutherford

*'What I have to offer sometimes seems so frail compared to the
monolithic lies created by those who control our lives. They plan
death and destruction and are seen as respectable citizens while I
offer my love and creativity and am made to feel like an outcast.'*

Penny Rimbaud

*'The only way to deal with an unfree world is to be so absolutely
free that your very existence is an act of rebellion'*

Albert Camus

This final chapter is somewhat of a reality check. Hopefully it can
help us clarify a few things as a well as giving us more inspiration
and reassurance.

A Paean, Not a Panacea

As we now know, wild spirituality alters our perspective on the nature and purpose of our (apparent) incarnation. Yet the realisation of our inherent Oneness isn't a cure for all ailments. Unlike some 'mind, body and spirit' guides that subtly blame the victim, telling us that *we create our own reality,* this book won't make you feel a failure for still having physical, mental or emotional problems. Instead it reminds us that life's a story and encourages us to affect change by being fully aware of our creative authorship.

We can't hope to make a difference, either to our life-story or anybody else's, when we don't understand the role of the illusion. The struggles of our (apparent) incarnation certainly make little sense when looked at from the angles most commonly taken:

1. *We're here to play out our 'karma'* – what goes around comes around and our current suffering reveals how wrongly we've behaved in other lives.
2. *We're here to suffer* – an outside Deity has deemed us sinful and unworthy, so we have to prove ourselves by humbly accepting our earthly punishments. Only then will heavenly rewards be forthcoming.
3. *We're here to create a perfect reality* – it's our fault if we can't fashion an abundant and miraculous life for ourselves.

To answer the first point – karma – let's consider some of those suffering now, such as the physically/mentally impaired and those living in extreme poverty/deprivation. If we observe them, not their limitations, then we'll find the most adversely affected beings have the strongest helping of wild essence within them. Their spirit shines out, undaunted by its temporary fetters, because it *remembers* who and what it truly is. This shows us that they've elected to experience severe restrictions *in order to teach others a gentle lesson* – perhaps about tolerance or patience. *Our lives aren't just for us* and those most in touch with their eternal self realise this. So, afflicted people aren't enduring handicaps because of any previous wrong doing – they're helping us all!

The notion of 'karmic debt payment' relies on the notion of chronological lives – incarnation as a progression along a timeline – and as such is inherently flawed. Time is an artificial construct that doesn't apply beyond the constraints of physical life. Yes, there're other lives/selves to experience through our particular perspective. When we're All Possibility how could there not be? But no doubt these happen *simultaneously*, in the eternal unfolding *Now*. Our life-stories are only witnessed singularly and chronologically for the sake of coherence, giving the familiar framework of beginning/middle/end. Without this we'd literally lose the plot. Think of a film – a fictional life-story – on a DVD. We prefer to watch it from start to finish to glean the narrative's meaning. Yet if we choose we can select scenes, freeze frames, repeat the bits we enjoy or take the DVD out of the player and examine the disc – the source – itself. Within that source disc *everything exists at once*. It's only our point of perception – where we focus our awareness – that anchors a scene at specific instant.

Our physicality is the player that allows the story to run from start to finish but our consciousness is the witness that realises this is an illusion and that all events happen concurrently.

We only appear to have life-story. It can be a trudge from one fixed point to another...or not. To address our second point, there's no cosmic penalty system involved and the only misery is caused by our *forgetting* that it's just a dream, and we're all the Dreamer. We're not here to score points or suffer in meek acceptance. Any trials and tribulations are tests we've set for ourselves to push our own boundaries and gain new insights. We're not supposed to be scratching away virtuously at paltry lives as to be eligible for a glorious hereafter. Nor are we meant to live in fear of being claimed by 'the dark side' because we're not as righteous and impeccable as we should be.

Because there are no sides; just our Self in different guises.

As we've considered, and may've experienced ourselves, there are *unseen* forces that are unscrupulous and devious. But they don't target us because we're lowly and sinful, rather because they are wayward – or naturally opposite to us – and we're *forgetful*. Being blamed for encountering a 'haunting', or attracting 'bad luck', is unhelpful to an already beleaguered individual. Instead, anyone that's 'psychically attacked' should be encouraged to accept the experience as valid, before ascertaining why it happened and what it means to them. Perhaps rather than being a pest, the tricksy *unseen* being is acting as a catalyst or rigorous teacher, pushing us to examine the nature of reality. There's a learning opportunity in every such incident, although we haven't got to indefinitely endure etheric interference to find it.

With our companion's help, and through the strength of our own *remembering*, we can deal decisively with the unwelcome attentions our *unseen* opposites, treating them as firmly but fairly as we would a salesman hawking unwanted goods on our doorstep. We can say *'no thank you!'* and be sure they'll not be there when we open the door again. Then we can assimilate what we've been taught, with absolutely no fear of being dragged off to a mythical place of damnation.

So, we've covered karma and suffering. Now let's look at the third point: the fallacy of creating a flawless life.

Reality Check

It can be said that *we create our own reality*:
* *We have free choice as to how we respond to any given circumstance* – we're *response-able*. We can experience the world unfolding in any way we wish but not manipulate it to fit our every whim.
* *We can affect change personally, locally and even globally* – a simple, soul-full act can trigger a chain of events and so we should never underestimate our role as 'part of the solution'. But this is *being the change we wish to see in the world*, rather

than intrinsically altering that world to suit us.

- *We're co-creators of an illusion* – all our personal life-dreams are interrelated and co-dependent. Creation isn't a series of self-contained units but an energetic, interactive, and responsive 'web of wyrd' we can work wisely with.
- *We're witnesses of a 'consensus reality'* – as individuals we've begun *remembering* but collectively we're still locked into the *forgetting*. Consequently the persistent illusion isn't necessarily the one we'd want. The more beings that *remember*, the more we'll have a shared wild dream, not a recurring nightmare.

As we've just begun to show, *we create our own reality* is a valuable starting point for discussion. Yet instead it of being a flexible springboard it's often hardened into an irrefutable tenet and its acceptance deemed essential to 'spiritual growth'. My initial problem with it is this: universal truth is just that – universal and *for all our relations*. If it can only be applied to privileged humans then it probably isn't an eternal absolute. As an animal in a factory farm, or an African child with the Ebola virus, can't be considered to be creating their own reality – rather dealing with the consequences of the 'consensus version' – then it doesn't hold up across the board....that is, unless we fall back on the tired notion of karmic retribution.

Tim Freke, the wonderful author and stand-up philosopher, is somebody who challenges all such received beliefs. He suggests that instead of expecting to affect major changes to the world we live in – forcibly moulding *What Is* into what we think should be – we gently plant 'intention seeds' with love, and see what happens. In his book '*How Long is Now?*' he says:

'*...Sometimes there's the impression that, if we could simply believe with enough fervour, we could create the perfect life. But it's not possible for all of our intention seeds to flourish. And believing that it's possible leads to a permanent feeling of inadequacy because we believe that we're failing to believe enough. The truth is that sometimes magic works and sometimes it doesn't... whether they* *become a reality depends on whether the world is conducive to them flourishing...'*

Tim's response illustrates that there's no substitute for intimate inquiry.

Our *unseen* companions can help us with all manner of philosophical issues, as well as guiding us on the best course of action to take for planting those intention seeds.

Let's call this our wild magic.

Naturally Enchanting

This generous, untamed magic has nothing to do with determinedly controlling events.

Nor is it to do with black, white or even green witchcraft. It's our birthright and available to *everybody at any time*; not just gleaned by the select from a secret society or religious belief system.

Wild magic is elegantly life-enhancing. It flows gracefully with the life-force, not pushing it around. It's about focussing our energies effectively – *everything is energy and our energies are everything* – to affect the natural current sensitively. To do this ,we use intent – our 'wish and will' – and we do it unfailingly *for the good of the All.* Not by demanding, but gently and firmly aligning ourselves with the best possible outcome, *whatever it may be.* We're guided into making this right alignment by our beneficent *unseen* companions who have the bigger picture, as well as our best interests at heart.

As with all else we do, magic's a collaborative endeavour.

To work wild magic we combine the imaginative, visionary faculties we used to build our wild sanctuary together with symbolic physical action. We can combine the power of our Infinitely Conscious, and infinitely considerate, Creator Self with the efforts of our everyday material aspect to make a coherent and potent magic. As I experienced in my cycling vision, the *unseen* realms, and our (apparently) dense 'ordinary reality', are both

energetic. They differ only in the frequency of their vibration...
and so in our ability to perceive them. An acceptance of the
energetic nature of existence is essential to successfully planting
those intention seeds in the world, in harmony with the seasonal
currents/rhythms of life.

To make an informed decision on what to 'plant', and to
discover when and how, I suggest we follow these guidelines.

1. Inner consultation with our *unseen* companions

With their access to the 'bigger picture' our guiding mentors can
help us identify:

a) What course of action is right in this particular *Now*, both
for our physical and our eternal self

b) How this choice will affect any manifest or *unseen* being
close to us

c) How it may affect the wider world/other realms

Once we have a clear idea we can weigh up the pros and
cons of any potential course of action. *If it harm none* is often
expressed as a guideline. Yet can it be possible to harm no other
when there're so many other realms, some containing those who
find our very existence an anathema? Also we inadvertently hurt
other beings just by walking on the earth, even by breathing.
Consequently we have to accept that in our current physical
guise we're never going to be perfect – or perfectly acceptable to
everyone – therefore accidental/incidental harm may result from
our existence. We can only hope for damage limitation, aiming
to consciously cause the least pain/disruption possible... *for the
good of the All.*

If we consider our choice to be as a stone dropped in a pond
then those closest to the splash will have the deepest effect and
so deserve our greatest consideration. As the ripples spread out
they'll lose potency until the edge of the pond barely registers
anything. If our act is inherently generous then we'll always do
more good than ill.

2. **Harmonious Alignment with Natural Forces**

   Now we turn our attentions to the prevailing natural tides. Which phase or time best suits the resonance of our wish? Is our dream about beginnings, renewed growth, latency or a pulling back? We can align the principal energy of our wish with corresponding times of day, months, seasons, moon phases, planetary alignments, topographic features or weather conditions.

3. **Focussed Intent/Deep Imagining**

   Then we decide how we'll dwell on our will and wishing. Will we visualise/imagine what we want or use prayerful soul-poetry to evoke and invoke the dream?

4. **Appropriate Action/Representation**

   Finally we can decide how to represent our desired outcome *symbolically*, using music, imagery or handmade/natural/personal items. We can also choose a gifting to the land/beings involved – it could be food/drink, bright jewels/charms, ribbons or perhaps a service like cleaning up a stretch of rubbish-strewn river bank.

5. **Right Outcome**

   Wild magic isn't an exact science. We're working with *energies*, not bricks and mortar, and even a well-built wall can crumble due to unforeseen influences. There're always unexpected prevailing forces. Fates and futures – or whole realities – shift and are mutable. That's why we've a chance of influencing them... but also why we may not succeed. If conditions are favourable and our intent/actions are aligned, a subtle yet potent influence will be experienced. Perhaps not immediately, and perhaps not how we expect, but we must trust our emanation will find its own best way of expressing itself.

   And that's it! It's not as complicated as it sounds and once we've got the formula we'll be working wild magic instinctively and seamlessly as a part of our lives.

   Here's an actual example of how it all comes together.

162

Where the Heart Is

My friend needed to move to a place that would be conducive to his health and creativity as both were suffering in a damp, cramped flat. His companions confirmed this was what he needed and said they'd help with identifying the best place for him at that time. Their guidance was quite specific and they suggested a local area for him to focus on, somewhere he recognised and already liked.

Then he considered the flow of the seasonal energy for his endeavour. He needed a burgeoning, flourishing energy to carry his dream of a nurturing home to fruition – that of spring/ summer, dawn to midday or waxing to full moon. Then every morning he began passionately chanting for the right home for himself. While he chanted he repeatedly visualising himself leaving his empty flat, posting the keys through the landlord's letterbox and moving off in the hired removal van.

Then, at sunrise on a bright spring morning – and when the moon was waxing – he went to plant a symbol in his desired neighbourhood. He buried some of his freshly cut hair and finger nail parings. Symbolically these offerings expressed that *he'd* be rooted like a seed; *he* would grow well there. Then he 'watered' his buried symbols with his own saliva and offered some actual seeds for the land and its denizens...and so *for the good of the All.*

My friend was swiftly offered a new flat in the same area he had buried his symbols of intent, and all before midsummer. He's much healthier in his new home and, as promised, he's committing his renewed energies to revealing nature's beauty through photography. His new landlord has a reliable tenant and the people that share his block have a considerate neighbour.

All is well.

Of course all of this could've been achieved just by *entering the silence*. When we align with Infinite Consciousness we're immediately in tune with All Possibility and so our highest good. By consistently making this connection we'll find that life naturally becomes enchanted, meaningful and totally *on the One*. But sometimes going through the procedure we've just discussed helps us to pull focus in a light-hearted, creative way. It's fun as long as it doesn't become too ritualistic. Ritual is yet another way we distract ourselves from the simple eloquence of *What Is*. We can enjoy the process, and the symbolism, but always know the real magical interaction happens quietly, one-to-One, and beyond all transient props and trimmings.

Like wild spirituality, wild magic isn't a panacea for all ills or an escape route from our life-lessons. It's just a way of enhancing life. If circumstances are favourable and we've made informed and sensitive choices, then there's no reason why we can't make things a little sweeter.

In an Ideal World

Can there ever be a faultless reality? We may think the *remembering* would create one here on Earth yet perhaps this particular manifest realm needs contrast, both for definition and to learn how not to be. As the visionary William Blake put it, '*without contraries, no progression. Attraction and repulsion, reason and energy, love and hate are necessary to human existence.*'

This doesn't mean we should be horrible just to provide contrast, rather that we should appreciate all variations on the theme of life for what they offer. Our Greater Self has no partiality, only acceptance, while our small 'me' self adores Indian food, loves modern jazz and detests the colour green. To deny that we feel favour for some things and antipathy for others is to negate our particular experience. Preferences are interesting, and individualisation to be enjoyed, but not be engulfed or hoodwinked by.

Just as difficulties are to be welcomed, not feared, as they provide opportunities for growth.

We can't opt out of all life's valuable lessons. We set them for ourselves on a deeper level and so 'willing and wishing' them all away would be counter-productive. Trying to sidestep difficulties is like deferring exams we need to take in order to proceed in our chosen subject. Stalling makes tests seem insurmountable and so our resistance grows. If we accept that they're part of this reality, assisting us in becoming better expressions of All-That-Is, then we're much better served. This means losing our belief that everything should be smooth in our lives. The ups and downs can be accepted as what makes a journey – or a good tale – interesting. As we know, there're ways we can live well in spite of any difficulties.

And perhaps we can gain some comfort in our difficult times by remembering that the harder the lessons, the more intrepid the student.

End of Term

No student in this life-school of ours ever fails. They may not perform up to their own expectations, feeling they didn't try hard enough or made poor choices, but there's no absolute failure.

There're so many variations of approach, or learning styles, in life and none of them completely correct...only more or less effective for us. When we abandon the notion that there's an 'external adjudicator' eyeing us vigilantly then we can find value in any experience. Nobody ever reached their death bed and wished they'd worried harder, only that they'd loved deeper and had more fun, regardless of their hardships. Despite what we may think now *we never set ourselves more than we can cope with* and with that in mind we can relish the challenges we've set ourselves.

We all have wobbles as part of our development. If we're feeling resilient and focussed then our troubles can assist us in becoming wiser, kinder or braver, following the maxim *whatever doesn't kill us makes us stronger*. But if the support isn't there – or we believe it isn't – then our difficulties overwhelm our system and make us 'crash'. It's at this point we can wait it out to see if we 'reboot' naturally or we may want to 'pull the plug' on our 'body computer'. When we take our own lives, we switch ourselves off rather than waiting to be switched off. If we leave with awareness, in full *remembering*, then the soul-information stored on our 'body computer' goes back into the 'Internet' of the All. If we leave in distress or confusion – in a *forgetful* state – then we may linger in a forgotten file, not accessed but not deleted either. There are *unseen* helpers to assist our release from this state but it's better not to put ourselves there in the first place.

Those of us who choose to opt out of life early may feel temporary relief in the freedom from an overloaded, crashing 'body computer'. Yet on reflection we may be disappointed in our lack of tenacity or resourcefulness in finding a solution. *But that's all.* There's no punishment for those who choose to 'shut down' early, except by their own self. Because there's no authority but ourselves: Our Self. Self-torment is a choice we can make, or not.

Human emotions only apply if we determinedly stay within the human mindset, even though we're actually free of it. Identifying with those emotions is like pure information wanting to be downloaded by an old glitchy computer. Without identification we can be kind to our human mistakes, reviewing our life-story with generous compassion, just as we'd support a friend performing in a difficult play. In so doing we can appreciate where we acted well and what could be improved upon. What's important is accepting we tackled the lessons to the best of our ability at that time. Our eternal wild aspect understands it's all about learning and nothing to do with success or failure.

Whoever heard of a successful colour? Or a failed jellyfish? Success and failure are two ends of a stick that we beat ourselves with unnecessarily. And we can just as easily reject the stick.

The competitiveness and one-upmanship of the *forgetting* fosters the misery that creates suicides. *Remembering* frees us from such terrible restrictions and allows us to support each other through the manifest experience, come what may. Until we do this, humanity will continue to be in the painful state of competitive separation that claims many casualties along the way.

The separation of our current 'consensus reality' makes for a life-school that's absurd at best, distorted and disturbing at worst, and we shouldn't berate ourselves if we find it so. Modern mainstream society is such a mixed up place it's a miracle we can cope at all when we're pitched headlong into it. Some do grasp the skewed rules of this 'virtual game' quickly and adapt to its challenges, while others – sensitive wild spirits – feel overwhelmed and are blamed for not keeping up. It's a relief to stop berating ourselves for finding it upsetting and perplexing and instead have permission to realise society as deranged and inadequate...not us.

The structure of our life-school has warped and degenerated so that we're plunged into a mad house of Orwellian contradictions.

It's honest, not negative, to make such an observation about our chosen 'classroom'. As this book is all about authenticity it seems pertinent to discuss those things that're passed off as normal every day while actually being aberrant. It's one thing to set ourselves challenges in the apparent manifest realms but to condone the unreasonable as acceptable isn't beneficial to anyone. In fact it fosters the sense of failure that's so detrimental to our real eternal development. I believe these aberrations should be highlighted for what they are. Only then we can decide what would be the better 'consensus reality' for us all.

Let's think of it as the reform of our education system.

The Madness of King Human

Self-hypnosis teacher and author Michael Ellner says *'just look at us. Everything is backwards; everything's upside down'*.

What follows are some examples of the insidious topsy-turvy madness we're in the grip of whilst being assured of its sanity. It patently isn't! When we've read it we'll no doubt add more points of our own because once we begin to examine the version of reality we've been sold, we tend to see its craziness everywhere. This list isn't designed to make us despair, or even get angry, but to enable us to be less harsh on ourselves when we feel frustrated or disheartened. We're living in a system which we're told is right, while we're wrong and need fixing...and that simply isn't true. It isn't we who are failing but the defective construct we've found ourselves caught up in; one we didn't make or want but which we're made to adhere to none-the-less.

As Jidda Krishnamurti said '*it is no measure of health to be well-adjusted in a profoundly sick society*'.

Alone we may not have felt able to challenged society's sickness. Now we can gain validation and feel empowered to act wisely and well, not as a *reaction against* but as a considered *response to*. We may not have made the problem but it's ours to solve now – part of our creative life-challenge. To this end I've included a few simple alternatives to each point. These may be obvious but answers can elude us when we're struggling to make sense of things. I'm sure that together we'll dream up many more viable solutions for a sustainable, compassionate future. It's just a case of making a start.

Here are some observations to begin the process.

1. **Mean Green**

   In England we dedicate vast expanses to grass. Not wild grass that supports flora and fauna but cut-to-within-an-inch-of-its-life grass that has no purpose but to neatly provide a backdrop for human enjoyment...a sort of natural picnic rug. These bright green, but strangely barren, areas are our lawns, verges and parks. Places that could thrive and create abundance but by some unspoken agreement have been consigned to a sterile tidiness.

   Most gardens are restrained rectangles, perhaps with a regulatory row of bedding plants kept rigorously weed-free. Each tamed patch begs the question *who's this for?* Gardens are an opportunity to care-take a mini nature reserve yet we have them for display purposes only, letting them demonstrate our worth as upright citizens. Some even go as far as to concrete or gravel over that unruly grass altogether.

The rented house I now live in has this loathsome gravel. I'd have the stones removed but it's beyond my resources, so I've let the wilful dandelions, cleavers, nettles and thistles – those supposed weeds – push up willy-nilly. Flies, bees, and beetles find this to their liking. I'm waiting for the complaints about the state of my garden any day now. But tidiness isn't my priority; untamed nature is.

Do our gardens reflect our understanding of the wild world or our aversion to it?

Similarly our shared expanses are mowed down to the equivalent of a buzz cut with military precision. A hospital I attend is surrounded by large, but entirely empty, open space which could grow organic vegetables, wildflowers and native trees. These could be tended by patients and visitors: great natural therapy that'd encourage vital healing connections between people and place. To prove this is possible, the town of Todmorden in the north of England has sowed its communal areas. As part of the 'Incredible Edible Todmorden Unlimited' project fruit and vegetables are free at any time, planted and picked by the people. In the West we seldom make any personal connection with our means of sustenance. We import vegetables; mostly out of season, not organic and wrapped in plastic packaging. Yet in Todmorden that essential link between the season, the process involved and what appears on a plate is made effortlessly, every day.

Gardens can be shared and every available window box, verge, roundabout, balcony or concrete yard planted. Not to impress anyone, or even to grow healthy food for people, *but for life itself.* We're not just consumers but consummate co-creators.

169

The greening of our country lies with the ordinary, extraordinary person who has joyfully rewilded themselves and the area they care for. What a shame then that those with custody of vast swathes of our land – the big landowners and farmers – wantonly abuse it.

2. Cultivation of Bad Habits

There's nothing refined about industrialised agriculture, a system which defies every natural law relating to food growing and good stewardship. Rather than being thriving areas supporting nutritious crops, the majority of our farmed fields are essentially dead – poisoned into submission.

I currently live in Wiltshire, a big farming county, and regularly see the 'sprayers' out covering the fields. I'd hoped that what was being sprayed was natural fertiliser but I recently found a cache of discarded 'agri-chemicals' leaking in a ditch. One of these – the blithely named 'Fandango' – was manufactured by the same people that brought Zyklon B to Nazi Germany, and the other – the equally jauntily named 'Gala' – by the company linked to both Agent Orange and the Bhopal disaster. Both paradoxically urged safe disposal of the containers and their contents. I also observed a tank covered in hazard warnings to guard from dangerous leakages from the toxic contents...liquid to be sprayed on the crops.

Need we look any further for an example of insanity than this?

What goes through the minds of farmers who spray plants (plus soil and all non-human inhabitants) with these 'pesticides' whilst having to wear protective clothing? Perhaps they believe the land's been around for millennia so a drop of poison won't harm it. Perhaps they actually believe that if the Government's approved the chemical cocktail it must be safe. Perhaps they think *we've all got to die sometime*, dismissing their actions as part of the dog-eat-dog, survival-of-the-fittest natural world. Or perhaps they don't care at all.

Although I want to empathise with all beings, it's hard when their actions are so harmful.

But for all its harm, this systematic poisoning is recognised as 'conventional farming'. Natural – and genuinely conventional – methods are labelled 'organic' and considered somewhat 'fringe'. The idea of 'inorganic' food is disturbing yet we tolerate it. Monoculture – the hard and fast, high intensity/low diversity approach – is standardised and legitimised even though it means corrupted food, impoverished land and deprived wildlife. It's hard to imagine what earthly good can come of this system. It certainly isn't benefitting local people as, despite being surrounded by toxic arable land, I've yet to find a loaf made from locally sourced grain. In fact last year I discovered that wheat was harvested then left to rot in rat-infested piles on barn floors.

Clearly people aren't the only victims. Wild creatures have no choice but to eat 'inorganic' food – contaminated grass, grubs, small mammals etc. Their water is laced with a substance 'harmful to aquatic life'. But the wild food chain comes below business links because it provides cheap (in all senses of the word), mass-produced fare with maximum profit for the few.

Of course local unprocessed farming that supports bio-diversity is the only sane answer to a question that should never have to be asked. We each need to express our desire for unadulterated food that's grown close to home, buying as much as we can despite the inflated cost. Better still, let's grow as much as we can ourselves, withdrawing our support from sprayed crops. If our children are shown green ways by their elders – given access to soil, hands-on experience and an understanding of their part in natural cycles of growth and dying back, whilst being encouraged to *remember* their interconnectedness – then the abuse of the earth and its denizens will come to be seen as the vile mistake they are...

an embarrassing reminder of an unenlightened past.

Perhaps then the negligent 'custodians of the land' will be condemned as any other criminal who poisons, rather than given a government grant.

3. Living on the Hedge

There's not much of an escape for wildlife from our barren gardens or chemical-laden fields into our hedgerows. In a country where most things have been tamed within an inch of their lives, hedges should be 'edge-lands'; wild margins where a diversity of species can flourish unimpeded, finding good shelter and sustenance.

Yet almost as soon as the hawthorn, elder, blackthorn, wild rose and bramble have fruited, a machine is brought out along the lanes and roadsides which systematically hacks bushes and trees apart. This is as much proper hedge trimming as using a hatchet on a man's hair is good barbering. It leaves them brutally snapped, left vulnerable to infection. It removes food – nuts, berries, fungi, lichen, insects – and refuge from the species who need it in the coming winter. Machines also take away the fallen material rather than letting it go to the earth.

I wonder if the people who drive these mechanical mutilators along are the same people who bemoan the lack of songbirds?

Do all hedges need pruning? Unless they're obscuring a road sign, causing a hazard to pedestrians, or scraping cars then where's the problem? It's not about keeping the hedge healthy and strong so again it comes back to *neatness*...not a good reason to render a habitat uninhabitable.

Any trimming could be done by hand – respectfully, responsively and collectively, in local teams allocated a stretch to care for. This would help us bond with others in our locality in an easy, meaningful way. Tending a hedgerow would allow us to feel part of the wheel of the year, not passive bystanders to it. It'd re-establish our sense of place, fostering a sense of accountability in us beyond what's considered 'ours'. We'd be part of something worthwhile, not excluded as 'non-landowners'.

This may seem like a small issue, yet in such matters we set the tone. We need to have zero tolerance of any and all disrespect – and any insane behaviour – otherwise we become complicit. Any imprudence becomes the norm if unchallenged.

Just as our harmful energy dependency has.

4. Feeling the Force

How can people understand the vital link between themselves and the untamed aspect of being – or connect with the earth they live on – when the majority of houses are sealed units, bombarded by electro-magnetic signals and entirely (and unconsciously) reliant on something that's deleterious to the wider – wilder – world.

Fossil-fuelled electricity.

One of the most telling features of this crazy dependence is that most new houses are built without a chimney. These chimney-less dwellings appear in once flourishing areas and are named – either with a total lack of irony or phenomenal callousness – 'The Spinney' or 'Willowbrook' for the very feature they've replaced. Rather than nestle naturally into the land they sit in regimented blocks – each a fortressed island full of artificial materials and plugged resolutely in to the mains.

It isn't only new houses that're chimney-less. Many apartments or flats never have them with while older houses have blocked theirs, perhaps situating a boiler there and installing a reproduction fire in the hearth. This replacement is perhaps one of the greatest signs of our incipient madness. Our lack of a chimney means that the majority of people have no way to heat their accommodation, or their food, if their power goes off...or runs out. Gas or oil fired central heating doesn't work without electricity. Mains water is reliant on it to be filtered and pumped. And this is before we go into the shops being unable to keep fresh food or take delivery of new stock – no power means no refrigeration or factory production. No power means no computers, no banks, no money...

It's all out of our control yet we act like we're organised. We're addicts in denial, pretending we're thriving in a functioning whole.

If we live in our own homes we can perhaps, if money allows, rectify our power dependency by installing wind generators, solar panels, wood-burning stoves, etc. We can get decent insulation to keep our heat in and turn our garden over to fruit and vegetables. In rented accommodation it's much harder to start converting things to suit our convictions or needs. As for water, most of us are completely dependent on the mains. The majority of our rivers are polluted beyond drinking. Some of us have natural springs nearby, or an ancient well, but most would have a hard job to satisfy the most fundamental human need if the taps ran dry.

We require creative joined-up solutions, not the straight-line separatist thinking that got us into this predicament.

Fossil fuels, nuclear power and wind farms all have serious drawbacks. With the world being approximately seventy percent water – echoing the percentage of water in an infant's body – utilising wave power seems our best chance, but only with a concerted desire to make it work, not a half-hearted dabbling. Yet there's also the 'free energy' proposition, as propounded by the genius Nikola Tesla. I urge the reader to research this free – or zero point – energy for themselves. The words *enlightenment* and *empowerment* will take on a whole new meaning. Free energy isn't that mysterious when we consider we're energetic beings living in an energetic reality, sustained by a vast burning ball of free energy – the sun.

The real mystery is why we're still in the dark ages when it comes to utilising power.

The flourishing 'transition towns' network in the UK aims to pool resources/ideas/expertise and do something practical to end our unhealthy dependency, planning a smooth conversion from dirty habits to healthy interdependence. Perhaps it's time for us to find our local group, or begin our own.

Because most of us don't yet have much support in our lives.

5. So Near and Yet So Far

No matter what the media tells us, our communities are not real communities. They're disparate collections of people who just happen to live in close proximity...and probably wish they didn't have to.

Try standing quietly in a local shopping area and observe human interactions. Yes, there're those who say hello or stop to chat. But most people behave as if their counterparts simply aren't there. If not considered directly relevant, or readily identifiable, people skirt around and scuttle past each other, heads down and gazes studiously averted. Of course this avoidance is far worse in a larger urban area. Looking at everyday behaviour, there's little sense of communality, let alone an appreciation that we're all Infinite Consciousness sharing an experience! Our non-human relations, such as pigeons, get even less acknowledgment.

We may as well be in different worlds for all the real relationship there is.

An exchange of platitudes about the weather, our companion dog or the winner of yesterday's match doesn't make a community. Nor does taking in a parcel or offering a child a lift to school. Yes, these gestures are important but if there's no shared vision, no collective ethos and *no deep sense of relationship under the skin,* then we're just separate units that happen to share a locality and interact superficially when it's convenient.

We're a polite society that keeps up appearances.

It's hardly surprising that our public life is more private than ever before. The housing estates where the majority of us live are a recipe for disaster; personally, collectively and in a wider ecological sense. Just as the countryside is bounded into parcels of owned land, all tied up tight with barbed wire, our residential areas are nothing more than tidy plots divided by six foot fences, gates and walls – the ubiquitous statements of 'mine' and 'separate' replete with competitive status symbols. We're boxed up neatly with 'our stuff'.

Of course there's another way to live, one beautifully demonstrated by an 'intentional community' named Tinker's Bubble in Somerset, UK. There, people have chosen to live together. Buildings are low impact temporary structures. Hand tools are used, unadulterated food is grown, and there's a ban of fossil fuels on site, saving paraffin for lamps. Yet creating such an alternative within society as it stands is becoming harder, with land more expensive and planning permission for anything unconventional made unattainable. Squatting is outlawed and travelling communities marginalised further. A deliberate repurposing of existing space is needed, but achieved peaceably, *en masse,* with absolute unity of purpose.

Reclaiming the land is important but so is reclaiming relationship, as without deep connectedness our plans will be shallow and lack longevity.

We can begin building relationships now. Let's ask retailers of local independent shops/markets to stock the things we'd like, rather than sourcing from Internet companies. Shopping for everything locally can be difficult on limited finances but buying one item regularly – and connecting with the staff as we do so – is investing in something we care about. Many of our towns have gone from being distinctive places to an 'Anywhere-ville' of chain stores. Villages have become 'drive throughs' full of holiday lets and weekend retreats, without so much as a post office. If we want to be part of a thriving whole we need to keep the unique heart alive.

Another area needing consideration is transport. Most of us take boxed up journeys in 'our' car, which reinforces the inside/outside, mine/yours paradigm. Certainly public transport can be woefully inadequate outside of our cities, forcing us into this position. Yet there's potential for a bespoke 'dial-a-ride' service, the likes of which is only currently available to the elderly or disabled. A prerequisite of taking our driving test could be dedicating time each year to a car sharing scheme. A directory in the local library could list each month's participating drivers and a computer database could make matches for us.

We simply need to shift our consciousness from 'me' to 'us' and from 'mine' to 'ours'. If we use 'Ours' in the largest, most encompassing sense, we've got the best chance of making a lasting difference, gladly taking responsibility for each other's wellbeing as parts of our own Self. It's not giving up our autonomy but expressing our individuality within a genuinely supportive web.

This is why allowing our children to explore Oneness is so important.

6. Foolish Schooling

Our education system perpetuates one-upmanship, promotes acquisitive achievement and is almost set up to fail.

In state primary schools the teacher is a 'jack of all trades', teaching across subjects whilst being outnumbered by their variously able pupils at an average to thirty to one. Most parents with two children have their work cut out to give them appropriate attention, stimulation and guidance. So how can one adult be responsible for the mental, emotional and physical wellbeing of thirty unique individuals for up to six hours a day? Teachers are made to feel this system is perfectly reasonable and that if they're struggling they're not up to the job.

Lessons are planned within a tight curriculum, geared towards the passing of assessments and executed on a low resource budget. This means pressure on staff and children begins immediately. And it continues – *wham bam, exam* – right through to choosing 'what we want to do in the world', and beyond. By the time young people get to University they'll be shackled to the system by both horrendous fees and a set way of thinking.

Clearly literacy and numeracy are essential, with creative communication and calculation forming the foundation of further exploration. But when a human being is at its most supple and receptive – and at its closest to the *unseen* realm it has just arrived from – we don't allow them the liberty to inquire about the nature of existence. We limit their experience to the physical, telling them that's all there is. Except when it comes to religious instruction, of course. Then they're asked to believe the unbelievable alongside their times table. As so many of us know, this early indoctrination is difficult to shake off: *a mindset can be for life, not just for Christmas.*

A child is a conduit for truth – and a natural teacher – but isn't encouraged to share what it innately understands with us. Instead we cram it with formulas, dates, rules, goals and dogma. We deliberately switch priority away from their fluid, spiritual aspect towards a 'hard-headed' left-brained inflexible approach. We don't expand but control them, shutting down their lyrical, mystical impulse and programming them for operation in a competitive system. Perhaps this closing down is the point, because if a child was allowed to *remember* they wouldn't tolerate our human-centric sectarianism and small-mindedness; they'd seem both laughable and obscene. To avoid a rebellion we keep them from the true wonder of themselves and others.

Our schools are a missed opportunity, yet we're made to feel ashamed for disparaging it as *we're lucky to have an education system at all.* One day we'll look back and wonder at how we starved children of All Possibility, training them merely to exist.

Then this deliberate limiting of a budding being will seem like the criminal damage it is.

To be qualified to teach at all we first need to *remember* ourselves. Otherwise all we're doing is establishing the *forgetting* in another generation, perpetuating fragmentation and competition. Then we can introduce our essential Oneness for discussion: that's Oneness as a concept, not another indoctrination. Exploring our eternal aspect in its broadest, most creative, empathetic sense can only be beneficial, even if it can't be 'proved' or quantified.

But if we know who and what we truly are, we'll realise how unhealthy our society is and understand the real cause of our dis-ease.

7. **Irrational Health Service**
How sick and skewed our healthcare is was demonstrated for me recently when I filled in a form for someone. The form required a list of their prescribed medications and each side effect they caused them. As I wrote it became clear that these side effects were *effects* – the tablets were creating worse ailments than the ones they were supposedly curing. This person had gone from being fit and healthy, but with anxiety and depression, to being uncomfortably overweight with high blood pressure, high cholesterol, blurred vision, a

shuffling gait, sexual dysfunction, memory loss and painful wheezing...as well as heightened anxiety and depression. Of course they were now on more medications to deal with these new conditions. I doubt their doctor understands how this chemical cocktail will affect them long term.

People become trapped in a loop of pharmacological dependency; sustaining an industry, not their well-being.

Everywhere in healthcare there're anomalies. Patients are denied genuinely helpful treatments on financial grounds. Our hospitals have food we wouldn't usually eat, let alone select as nutritious fare for convalescence. We treat cancer by bombarding the body with radioactive poison. We accept that vaccinations containing mercury and other deadly toxins protect children. Today's children are test subjects in a crazy experiment, ingesting chemicals from food, water and air while dealing with an electro-magnetic 'soup' of signals from phones, wi-fi, etc. They're completely overloaded, including their exposure to deliberately fast-paced, strident television. Then we wonder why they can't cope with school – a comparatively slow-paced, unstimulating environment where they're expected to be quiet and concentrate. Those who can't are inevitably diagnosed with autistic spectrum disorders or ADHD. Sadly most of us now know somebody diagnosed. If autism is a genetic condition then why are cases sky-rocketing?

Yet we ignore the real problem and 'cure' the child with more chemicals.

We foster health problems with our artificial environments then test potential remedies on animals instead of using the more accurate – and less abhorrent – means available. The campaigning organisation Animal Aid suggests research using donated organs and tissue, cell cultures, micro-dosing, and computer modelling among other viable methods of clinical study. Organisations such as The Dr. Hadwen Trust make this humane research their priority.

Any cure founded by the pain of another being is no cure at all. There's no end to suffering unless all suffering is ended.

To bring deep, lasting healing the bigger picture is needed, with individual and collective causes/effects studied in a holistic approach. This takes time and means redefining *conventional medicine*. Are natural, traditional remedies really 'alternative' or are they (rather than fast-acting pharmaceuticals) what's normal? Healing is surely a gentle process, undertaken in relationship with the beings of seed and root – the willing green helpers. Yet we're driven to want an instant fix, because illness is inconvenient and creates 'an economic drain'.

And in this system 'the economy' dictates our entire lives.

8. Uneconomical Truth

Money doesn't really exist – it's an illusion within the illusion of life – yet we're in thrall to it, made miserable or happy by it, and often give our lives to it. How can it not exist when it sits in our wallets? Well, ultimately our wallets don't exist either!

But even within the framework of our physical reality, money is a deception.

Think of how a few noughts could be added to a bank account online through a computer hacker's wizardry. Does our statement actually tally to a manifest sum of notes? How can what's loaned be many times what's physically deposited, then interest charged on this inflated sum? It's all smoke and mirrors, with the trickery at our expense.

Really the only difference between our money and Monopoly money is our belief that one has worth and the other doesn't.

Our coins don't have much value, as gold or silver apparently do. They're not edible, can't be worn, don't provide shelter. They're just part of a false construct called 'the economy'. For this economy to flourish, products must be manufactured that nobody needs to consume. We, 'the consumer', must be convinced we want them by other industries, including advertising and fashion. Products range from hair gel to a factory-farmed chicken to flame-retardant curtains to a pop singer.

Frequently the country we live in doesn't make its own products but imports them, thus contributing to 'the world economy'. Entire regions can thrive or fail on the vagaries of 'market forces'. Individuals depend on this pointless continuum in order to pay their mortgage/rent, feed their families or gain any respect. They have to buy into a destructive construct that stresses them while damaging the planet and its inhabitants because others have too much invested in the charade to let it go.

This is the most incredible insanity, sold to us as normality. Many of us realise this yet we're stuck in the system, at a loss for how to extract ourselves.

Here's an example of this madness.

Consider the shops before Halloween. Twenty years ago the 31ˢᵗ of October was marked with a few ghost stories; now a whole industry's sprung up 'to fill a gap in the market'. There're plastic masks, synthetic wigs, tawdry outfits, luminous confectionary...a slew of poisonous tat. And come the 1ˢᵗ of November this deadly surplus is reduced to clear. Bought or remaindered, it's still destined for landfill as it won't be kept for next year. Reusing wouldn't keep the economy going; we need to manufacture more to keep people in jobs. At this is before we even consider Christmas...

Now imagine this scenario on a larger scale, with electrical goods, sofas, cars churned out ad infinitum, creating mountains of unbiodegradable things. Child labour and sweat shop slavery keep the prices low for us while mineral deposits are removed from the earth, trees felled, cows killed...

Enough! We've enough stuff.

Instead of buying into this big lie, let's only buy new things we genuinely need, like underwear. The rest can be 'pre-loved'. There's far more satisfaction locating what we want as a bargain in a charity shop or at a car boot sale. We can cherish what we have and fix it when it breaks. If we don't need it we can swap it, give it away on local 'free-cycle' networks or donate it to good causes. We can recycle what isn't reusable. The Strauss family of the Forest of Dean, UK, are a great example of what can be achieved. They reduced their throwaway waste to just a carrier bag full in one year.. For inspiration their website it www.myzerowaste.com

In Greece people have had financial hardship foisted upon them. This has forced them into successfully establishing barter systems in order to trade what they have, grow, make or do. Other places have set these schemes up voluntarily, trading within a credit system based on actual goods and services, not money. The ethos of 'make do and mend' has begun to creep back after a long hiatus, ostensibly as a 'lifestyle option' but offering genuine possibilities. Yet first we need to make the mental shift, understanding the system as it stands as a false, self-serving and unsustainable construct. Then rather than us cowering under the threat of impending fiscal disaster, the farce known as 'the economy' can to be deliberately collapsed by the people.

We need to realise the real power in this world...ours. Before it's too late.

9. All's Well That Ends Well?

If we need any more proof of society's insanity then we need look no further than our approach to death. Of course, there's really no such thing as death, only the casting off of the costume our character wore in its life-drama. But our society is still a way from grasping this truth and so believes in a physical demise as an ending – one that has to be dealt with in the most decorous way possible.

Recently I saw a hearse containing an ornate wooden coffin smothered with lavish floral tributes. Most likely that expensive edifice was destined for the flames of the crematorium. There the tragi-comedy would unfold with a quick ceremony (the next people are always waiting) with the coffin being tastefully shrouded by curtains as it vanished. Then the person would be incinerated, leaving ashes (fragments) for scattering. Or perhaps the coffin would be buried in an orderly cemetery plot. Then the body would have its natural decomposition delayed by poisonous chemicals and absorption into the earth hampered by the varnished casket. The burial service itself might be centred in a religion that neither the deceased, nor their mourners, has had any connection with...just because it's the done thing. In either case, any public mourning would be seemly with everything held in check to avoid embarrassment.

The way we deal with death is as artificial and sterile as the lives we lead. It sweeps what's painful under an extremely clean carpet, removing us from the visceral, untamed aspect of being. It could be said that when a loved one 'drops their robe' and passes on we don't need to worry about 'the gory details' involved. Yet surely we've gone too far in handing responsibility to the professionals? Death has become another commercial industry with florists, undertakers, casket makers *et al* selling us slick ready-made solutions.

The so-called 'green burial' provides a wilder way. Then our cast-off body's interred on designated land in a readily degradable shroud, a cardboard coffin or a woven willow casket. There are courses offering the opportunity to make our own in advance. The grave site isn't usually marked by an ostentatious stone – one that probably cost the earth to quarry – but by plants that meant something to us. The accompanying ceremony can be bespoke, rather than the standard version with its 'stiff upper lip' approach. Certainly there're a lot of us humans to bury in such a 'green' way but with our endless capacity for ingenuity, this problem could be creatively and considerately overcome.

I'm sure that most of us would prefer to sustain new growth like this, rather than be toxically boxed or unceremoniously burned. If so we need to express our preference, discussing it openly with our loved ones. Sadly this more natural way doesn't yet come cheap, and may not be available in our area, but it's worth looking into and asking for.

Again the 'organic' option is considered 'fringe' while what's unnatural is called conventional. We all need to challenge this and not settle for something we find objectionable as our life's final statement.

If we unflinchingly embrace our true eternal nature we can honour the passing of the outworn material aspect in a more befitting, wholesome way; one that respects the body's connection to the soil...and to the All. We'll act without a fear of endings or decay, and with a healthy disregard of man-made propriety.

Every life-story deserves a good, well-plotted ending.

Of course, there're always more signs of our collective madness.

- *Why do non-violent animal liberators receive custodial sentences longer than those of rapists?*
- *Why do we cut and import flowers, displaying their corpses in our homes rather than enjoying wild ones alive, in situ?*
- *Why is microwave weaponry discussed by 'experts' as dispassionately as they'd consider a new hat?*
- *Why do those doing the most vital work - caring for the elderly and disabled - get the lowest wages?*

And so on.

All of these issues can be addressed with our *unseen* companions, as they're as dedicated as we are to changing damaging human constructs. As our *unseen* guides are once-removed from physicality, they can bring clarity beyond the clouds of our tempestuous emotions. Yet even as we notice more of these crazy discrepancies, let's not concentrate on them. Instead let's focus on being the best person we can be in an imperfect world – the sort of honest, responsive person that makes up a more considerate reality.

Being the change we want to see is always the most effective activism.

Spare A Little Change, Please?

Recently I gave some valued possessions to be sold for a worthwhile cause. At first this made me feel virtuous but then I found myself pondering the efficacy of my actions. Why should I give things up when others with more money/influence could help without any such sacrifice? In such a tumultuous, unsympathetic world what could I achieve, and would it ever be appreciated? I had similar grudging, ungenerous thoughts when I became vegan, resenting the inconvenience of finding different meals to everyone else whilst paying more them. It seemed like a punishment, not a privilege…an obligation, not a loving offering.

Obviously having such thoughts made me feel uncomfortable, then ashamed. Dismayed at my own pettiness I gave myself a spontaneous piece of guidance:

Be bigger than you think yourself to be.

With that I realised that as long as I was concerned with the values of the *forgetful* world – being concerned with its responses even as I disparaged it – I'd be grudging and grasping. I'd be 'little me' operating solely from a limited perspective, seeking individual recognition because that's what society seems to reward. This 'little me' fearfully holds the eternal 'big me' back, stopping us from expressing our noblest attributes without conditions. It's like the small man who bullies to seem more powerful, knowing no other

186

way to survive in a competitive world. Yet 'big me' is actually always in control, letting 'little me' think it's the boss whilst calmly and compassionately witnessing its foot-stamping follies.

When we recognise our 'little me' in a world of other fearful 'little me's' then we're free to relinquish it. We can cease to ask *'what's in it for me?'* replacing it with *'what's in it for us?'* Imagine if such empathetic relating was the norm in a gentle, playful and mutually supportive realm! Such a reality wouldn't be dull or homogenised, rather a creative place where we could explore All Possibility without rivalry; freely being the inventors, dramatists, philosophers and artists we are. If this can be imagined then it can *be*. All dreams start with the dreamer. But first the dreamer has to get lucid and take control of the nightmare.

No more bad dreams. It's time to think big and be bigger.

Rise and Shine

Until the Great Reunion, there'll always be those who're waking up to their interconnectedness...and those who are so soundly asleep as to appear comatose. These sleepwalkers can commit heinous acts in their nightmare of separation and so deserve our empathy, just like any other suffering creature. Those in the middle of deep sleep and wakefulness have flashes of insight, becoming conscious sporadically. It's the role of those of us who are awakening – struggling to lucidity when numbing slumber beckons – to wake the others along with us. Not by issuing demands and badgering, but by living as we know we should. By this we're more like the sound of woodland birdsong than a shrill alarm clock.

It's a difficult job but someone's got to do it and as you and I are sharing these words together now, it may as well be us.

If not us, who? If not now, when?

We've never been more needed in this movement towards wholeness. So, let's behave as if we *remember*; not just knowing it intellectually but by *being* our understanding.

187

No more excuses. No more divisions or diversions. No more hurting our Self. Because now is always the time. And we're the ones we've been waiting for.

'Now you see without your eyes,
Now you know without your mind,
Now you feel beyond your heart,
That you are me, and we are they,
And all are free
To be each other.'

From Inner Guidance

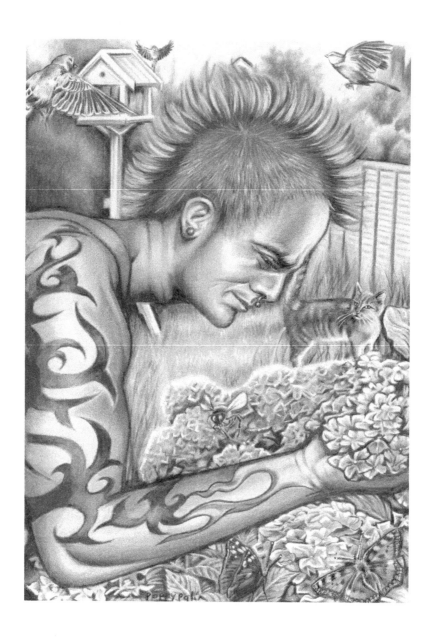

CONCLUSION
Homeward Bound and Free

'The highest of all is not to understand, the highest, but to act on it.'

Kierkegaard

'We had...grown bigger in the bigness of the whole.'

Ernest Shackleton

'I want you to...I want you to sense your own strength.'

E P Thompson

'Be a light unto yourself.'

J. Krishnamurti

By now we'll have a deep sense of our untamed, yet beautifully composed, way of being. We'll know ourselves as both trailblazers and discovers of what's been there all along.

We'll know that our wild way offers a way of uniting previously disparate strands – green mysticism, lucid living, spiritwalking, animal rights, eco-activism and a healthy helping of peaceful anarchism – to create a vital, autonomous yet wholly altruistic approach centred in empathy. No, it can't be scientifically validated or argued academically and it has no formal tradition. Instead it's entirely experiential and as universal as it is personal, proving its worth beyond all reason through endless compassion.

It's open-minded and like-minded, not single-minded. It minds from the deep green heart, not the head. Green-spirited is always the opposite of mean-spirited.

The pathless wild path has no rigid beliefs to divide us from those who don't believe. It takes no sides and knows no bounds. It has no chosen people, and belongs to every being – seen, *unseen*, human and non-human – equally. There are no masters, no Gods and no authority but our caring, incredible selves: the representatives of our Self. We're responsible for our own wholesome, care-full spirituality, expressed as nature intended – consciously, creatively and flexibly.

Our fresh awareness – our One-consciousness – means we're living by a unifying principle. We're *on the One*; in synch with the rich mystery and authentic magic of being, not tossed about on a sea of fate and external judgment. We can experience being One and one simultaneously, even as we stroke a cat, peel a potato or switch on our computer.

Ours is an everyday enchantment: down-to-earth and super-natural.

As individuals we matter and yet we don't matter at all, for we're not matter but everlasting energy seeking expression. By this realisation we live more light-heartedly but also more bravely, knowing there's nothing to lose and All-That-Is to gain. We trust in our own, and each others, generous Creator-nature and dance our part in the beguiling unfolding with more grace and subtlety than before.

We're being the love, soul-fully, and letting go of the rest.

Whichever way we go from here we've begun waking our innate wild spirit. It'll go on informing our lives, deepening our experiences and enlivening our responses, even if we temporarily retreat into apathy, fixed belief or scepticism. Our *remembering* – and so our part in the Great Reunion – will always continue in this precious shared *Now*.

And how shall we fill this *Now*? In active service to others? Spreading awareness? Following our creative bliss? Exploring all possibilities?

In whatever way as long as there's delight in it. Because wild spirituality isn't meant to be taken too seriously, even though it's the most important thing in the world.

As such perhaps its most fitting piece of guidance is found in the meaningful whimsy of an English nursery rhyme:

'*Row, row, row your boat, gently down the stream,*
Merrily, merrily, merrily, merrily; life is but a dream.'

Today it may seem as if we're soul-sailing against the tide. Or out on the tremulous limb of a solitary tree. Yet tomorrow we'll become aware that a forest of glistening green has lit into life all around us, leaf to bright leaf and bough to strong bough. We'll be as one living organism; the Oneness we truly are.

That glorious moment of unification will come sooner than we think; swelling to sweetness in the eternal Now. *We just need to dream harder – wilder – to bring it fully into being.*

Because everything is energy and our energies are everything.

So, this is where we appear to part ways. Of course I could continue. On a questing journey, delicious new insights reveal themselves every day. Trying to précis eternal truth, or express the ineffable, is both impossible and an ongoing labour of love. I yearn for the most apposite, evocative metaphor but always fall short of expressing the simple profundity and natural vivacity of my subject.

All Possibility confounds as much as it inspires.

If this book were tweaked indefinitely it would become more accomplished, but lose the fervour that generated it. And if I waited until I *remembered* everything before communicating, it would be dictated from beyond the grave. All I can offer is a tenderly crafted interim report – a snapshot of understanding, not a full and final statement.

A signpost on the journey, not another dead end.

There can be no real conclusion here. Our story is ceaseless, infinite; unfolding. I just offer you gratitude for your company thus far and wish you joy as we travel onwards, ever-connected but following our own shining course.

Onwards, inwards, outwards...*homewards.*

Go well...*for the good of the All.* For your journey is my journey. *Ours.*

You've read the book, now plant a tree

Printed in the USA
CPSIA information can be obtained
at www.ICGtesting.com
LVHW051959140923
758260LV00009B/250